SHUGENDO

The Ineffable Wakefulness of Nature

Shodo Koshikidake

CONTENTS:

FOREWORD

I first met Koshikidake san close to thirty years ago when I went to Mt Haguro in August 1994 to take part in the mountain entry retreat called the Autumn Peak (Akinomine) at Kotakuji. I had gone to Haguro for the first time two years earlier in 1992 at the invitation of Yamagata prefecture to take part in a "yamabushi experience" there. I was captivated by that experience, so different to the practice in a Zen temple that I had been doing for the previous fifteen years or so. The event had been organised by Hoshino Fumihiro, whose family had been head of the pilgrim lodging Daishobo for around three hundred years. He was then director of the Ideha Cultural Centre in Toge, a museum at the foot of Mt Haguro, and was passionate about bringing visitors to an awareness of the long religious tradition of the area.

However, this tradition had been broken in the nineteenth century, when Jakkoji, the shrine-temple complex on Mt Haguro, was forced to become a shrine and abandon its Buddhist and Shugendo heritage. In 1873 a religious bureaucrat called Nishikawa Sugao was sent from Tokyo to rid the complex of what he called old fashioned ways and superstition. It proved impossible to wipe the slate clean and he had to tempt especially high-ranking families like Hoshino's to accept the new order by making compromises with important Shugendo traditions, especially the Autumn Peak retreat. Hoshino's family gave their allegiance to the new shrine in 1874, and from then they occupied junior positions in the shrine organization and followed the revised ritual patterns and explanations that looked to Meiji Shinto constructions and obscured the Buddhist heritage. The "yamabushi experience" provided by Hoshino was deeply coloured by such revised interpretations, yet he and the mountain together left me wanting to know more about Shugendo.

In September 1993, at Hoshino's suggestion, I took part in a newly created practice at Dewa Sanzan Jinja called Miko Shugyo. Women were not allowed to take part in the Shrine's Autumn Peak. They had long asked to be included but there was considerable opposition to the idea from both within and without. Some said that breaking the ban on women would bring down the wrath of the kami on the shrine, while others rejected innovation per se, fearing unforeseen repercussions. In a form of reverse discrimination, one shrine yamabushi explained his opposition that it was not necessary for women to train in the mountain because they were already more spiritually powerful than men. The then head of the shrine, the late Abe Yoshiharu, who was a powerful force behind the instigation of Miko Shugyo, remarked to me that it was his impression that a good deal of the opposition was based on the fear that women's physical strength would be insufficient for yamabushi training, and further, their presence would distract male trainees if men and women trained together. When asked about the old rationale of female pollution, he said that such thinking was not fitting in the modern age and it was not a logical excuse, given that in ancient times women occupied a central role in ritual. Proponents of women's inclusion took the opportunity offered by the celebrations in 1993 marking the 1400th anniversary of the mountain's legendary founding to include a five day training period in late June, justifying the decision that it was in accordance with the will and compassion of its legendary founder, Hachiko Oji, and in response to the social changes in recent times that had brought women more to the fore.

Though Miko Shugyo was a contrived practice having only surface connections with the traditional form of the Autumn Peak, I am grateful to have had the opportunity to have been able to practise inside the Buchudo, the "Mountain-Entry Hall" at Fukugoshi about a mile from the Main Shrine on Haguro's summit. The seclusion rituals of the present Autumn Peak, conducted by Haguro Shugen Honshu and based at Kotakuji, its temple at Arasawa, were devised according to the layout of the Buchudo, a long rectangular building, with a shrine at one end and a large door in the middle of one of the long sides. As I was to discover, compromises had to be made both to the living arrangements of participants as well as to some ritual elements when constricted by a typical temple layout. I was also charmed to find reminders of the pre-Meiji past that have been lost in the modern Buddhist practice, like the custom of eating a skewer of five vegetables of different shapes called *gorinto* directly before leaving the Buchudo for the last time.

There was another outcome of Miko Shugyo that turned out to be life-changing for me. Abe san acted as daisendatsu, with the late Hoshino Mitsuo (Yoseibo) as his deputy (*doshi*). It was Yoseibo who showed us the headless statues near the Main Shrine on Haguro and explained what had happened as a result of the legislation to clarify Shinto and Buddhism (*shinbutsu bunri*), and who expressed his sorrow at the rift that had split Haguro Shugendo as a result. Wanting to bridge the divide, as a young man he learned the Hokke Senbo (Lotus Repentance Liturgy) that is the core of the recitational of the Autumn Peak, and when visiting his parishioners always carried the Heart Sutra to chant with them. I owe my deep interest in *shinbutsu bunri* and its consequences for Haguro Shugendo to Yoseibo's passionate concern that this policy had wrenched out its heart. When I went back a couple of months later to visit the area, I asked Abe san about what had happened in the 1870s, and he kindly gave me a copy of a manuscript diary written by Nishikawa Sugao at the time. This became the basis for my doctoral dissertation at Cambridge University in 2000.

Having tasted Shugendo through Miko Shugyo, I now wanted to experience the "true" Autumn Peak as practised by the Buddhist Haguro Shugen Honshu, and so it was that, at the introduction of Professor Suzuki Masataka of Keio University, I took part for the first time in August 1994. Though I say "true", in fact modern Autumn Peak practice, whether Shinto or Buddhist, represents many compromises. The modern practice has shrunk to seven days (it was once reputedly 75) at both temple and shrine, resulting in ritual contraction, while extraneous Buddhist liturgical elements were added over the centuries. On the other hand, Buddhist symbolism was removed and the liturgy rewritten in Shinto terms by the shrine after 1874, meaning the inherent symbolism of the ten realms of rebirth is underplayed, as are the ritual practices associated with it. The one practice enthusiastically retained by the shrine Autumn Peak is *nanban ibushi*, symbolising the hells. It is treated as an ascetic practice, performed after each liturgical session at night, not only during the first section of the mountain-entry, as traditional ritual manuals stipulate. It lasts up to three times the length of the temple practice and there is pride among participants at their endurance.

That August, I remember sitting in the train heading toward Tsuruoka and, seeing Gassan, feeling that I had arrived home. I was proud finally to be taking part in the Autumn Peak at Kotakuji. This pride took a new meaning when I took ordination in 2006 and added my name to all of those priests of the past, especially those whom I had "met" in accounts of their experiences in the 1870s, as well as those who had helped to preserve Haguro Shugendo into the twentieth century.

Because seating during *gongyo* is according to rank, it so happened that, though Koshikidake san was two years senior to me, each year we found ourselves sitting in more or less the same area. We talked a lot about Shugendo, about the tragedy of *shinbutsu bunri* and about the centrality of *shinbutsu shugo* (combinatory) ideas and practices in restoring Shugendo. Subsequently, when reviving his family temple, he set about bringing back combinatory ritual practices, such as the incense goma, as fully as possible, based on his family's ritual documents, nine of which he had published in 1999.

I have closely followed Koshikidake san's efforts to restore his family's temple and reconstruct its Shugendo practices and traditions. I share his feelings of sadness and loss about the distortions created by Meiji religious policy. And I commend his endeavours to bring Shugendo to an audience outside Japan. It will be very interesting to see if Shugendo can transcend Japanese cultural and religious borders, and in doing so, how it may do so while remaining true to those very limitations. I hope this book may bring English readers a knowledge of, and a deeper appreciation for, the delight that is Shugendo.

Gaynor Sekimori
Chimyoin Jikun
25 November 2022

Preface

我今見聞得受持

Light, visible –
but untouchable

Something lurks in the shadows of the human mind. Is it God, the Buddha, a monster? It is likely that all of them exist within our mind at some point. To seek out the truth, we may have to delve right back into human pre-history. It is certain that something is there, in our deep mind, behind our memories, stemming from time immemorial. Our fear of what might be with us in the dark, and our fear of being exposed for what we are by the light, may come from there.

Sometimes, what humans seem to be best at in this age is killing one another. With just one push of a button, hundreds or thousands — even millions —may die. The media tells us about the horrors rampant in the world every day. Our modern society has become rich with convenience, with products of every possible kind, but we still cannot reach the supposed utopia we are pursuing. Sometimes, it seems as though the world is a place filled with demons. What is this thing hiding within the depths of our mind? How should we live? What should we seek? What should we do? To learn the answer, we must seek it in another realm. This is our starting point on the journey to finding the answer to the riddle of our mind's inner world.

I made a vow to teach Shugendo to all, no matter where they were born. Surprisingly, there has been some interest shown overseas, but many come with skewed ideas, thinking, for example, that Shugendo is a religion of ninja or samurai. Many are attracted to the image of a mysterious power beyond ordinary human understanding.

On the other hand, in Japan, Shugendo is often caricatured and associated with cult-like behaviour such as strange chanting, standing under waterfalls, wandering around in the mountains and so on. Yamabushi, practitioners of Shugendo, are often reduced to villains and evil wizards in films. The true meaning of yamabushi is not widely known. All these images at home and overseas might reflect some aspect of reality. In my experience, Shugendo practitioners are treated as outcasts in Japan. However, it is also not uncommon to hear of yamabushi performing great deeds through their ritual prayer (*kaji kito*).

Shugendo was outlawed and prohibited by the Meiji government in 1872 as part of its move to "clarify" Shinto and Buddhism into distinct entities. The impact of this act still rings through today, with Japanese authorities denying the religious belief of Shugendo, which at its core is the combination of Shinto and Buddhism. An example of this comes from my attempt in 2005 to have my temple, Kannonji, registered as a religious institution. When I was going through the application, the officer asked me to choose which category of religious belief the temple belonged to. I answered that it belonged to *shinbutsu-shugo* (kami-buddha combination). The officer told me that such a category would not be accepted, and I was to select either Buddhism or Shinto. If the temple fell outside of these two categories, I would have to choose "various/miscellaneous teachings", a category usually reserved for new religious movements and cults. In spite of the 1400-year history of Shugendo, the authorities treat it as if it has no historical significance or legitimacy. Despite the assurance of full religious freedom, the authorities do not accept its existence.

Without an appreciation of history, you may not understand the significance of what I am talking about. First, I would like readers to understand that historical attempts to ban and control Shugendo have drastically altered it, and that modern Shugendo bears little resemblance to its original, pre-Meiji era form. The aim of this book is to offer readers a glimpse of the ancient thought of Shugendo and introduce my desire to see its revival.

智慧無礙

True Wisdom
Free from Obstruction
Brightens the Universe

I'd like readers to imagine a bento (lunch box) with its lid closed. It is a very old bento, over 150 years old. Can you guess its contents? Just by looking at it, it would be difficult to know exactly what it once held. We can say the same thing about Shugendo.

The Meiji-era banning and dismantling of Shugendo triggered a movement that saw the majority of Shugendo documents, buddha-images and temple complexes dismantled, burnt or destroyed. The destruction associated with the Meiji Restoration often left little of former Shugendo sites beyond stone walls, foundation stones, or the remains of old tracks.

Shugendo practitioners were forced to laicise, become Shinto shrine attendants or Buddhist priests. The only traces of Shugendo that remained following these acts of ravage were carried out secretly by those who on the outside conformed to the new rules in the guise of Buddhist and Shinto priests. The tenacity of Shugendo is evident by its widescale revival, continuing to this day.

No matter what scholars or academics on the subject say, the teachings of Shugendo are not imagination or fantasy. How can we truly understand Shugendo? The only way to know the Way is to follow the Way and revive the practices and rituals according to ancient tradition. This is the guiding principle of my practice and understanding.

In my family's archive of medieval and premodern Shugendo texts there is a manual outlining the doctrines and practice methods associated with Mt. Omine, a Shugendo heartland located within modern day Nara and Wakayama prefectures. The practices of Mt. Omine are known to be difficult and harsh, even to this day. Nevertheless, the ancient Ten Realms practice it was associated with continues today only at Kotakuji/Shozen'in, Mt. Haguro (Yamagata prefecture), where the ten-realms mountain-entry ritual lasts for nine days. In past centuries, however, mountain-entry rituals were held each season, and some may have lasted months. The demands of modern life no longer allow for these ancient rhythms of practice, and due to a variety of factors they were abbreviated. I want to say, however, that Shugendo's ancient methods are still important. I hope this gives you some idea of the situation that Shugendo has been facing and that this book will shed light on Shugendo as an ancient practice. Let's open the bento box.

WHAT IS SHUGENDO?

自我得仏来

Meeting the eternal Buddha
In my bright reflection

In ancient times, people relied on the mountains for their survival and mountains formed the backbone of their lives. Over time, mountains were sanctified. In Japanese mythology there is a story concerning Ninigi no mikoto, the grandson of the sun goddess, who is said to have descended from the heavens to the peak of Mount Takachiho. Many stories like this tell us that mountains were seen as liminal spaces where the boundaries between heaven and earth blurred, and as places where deities would descend. The ancient beginnings of kami-faith is based on this intersection between heaven, earth and human.

According to the official record, Buddhism was brought to Japan in 552. This resulted in a conflict between the Mononobe clan, an anti-Buddhist faction, and the Soga clan, a pro-Buddhist faction. The Soga clan came out on top, and since that time many aspects of ancient Shinto were assimilated into and shaped by Buddhism.

To highlight the combinatory belief system that emerged, I'd like to share some historically significant material as evidence. First, I would like to introduce the deity Kongo Sekisho Zenshin Uho Doji, regarded as a manifestation of the Buddha Mahavairocana as well as the original form (*honjibutsu*) of Amaterasu Omikami; the sun goddess of Shinto. This figure shows the sun goddess holding a wish-fulfilling jewel as well as a sceptre adorned with a five-story stupa, both Buddhist implements. This medieval statue, only about 4 cm tall, is a clear expression of the time when Shinto deities were completely enmeshed with Buddhism. Dating from the fifteenth century, it remains an important statue held by Koshikidake Kannonji temple.

With Buddhism's influence, mountains would gradually develop into sites of Buddhist training. Practitioners following the Dharma would enter the mountains as a place of practice. En no Gyoja, one of Shugendo's founding figures, was the prime example of this. My temple holds a precious wooden statue of En no Gyoja dating from the fifteenth century. It is a very realistic depiction.

Typical of mountains where Shugendo practice was undertaken are those in the Omine area, located between Nara and Wakayama prefectures. This area was also the site of En no Gyoja's practice. Three Buddhist divinities were enshrined in the Kumano mountains in this region: the Thousand-Armed Kannon (Avalokitesvara) Bodhisattva, which embodies the quality of compassionate skilful-means, Yakushi Nyorai, the Medicine Buddha, and Amida Nyorai who has vowed rebirth for all in the Western Paradise. These three buddhas demonstrate how Kumano became a place where common people made pilgrimage in order to alleviate their sufferings, heal their ailments and seek a peaceful death. At Tosenji temple in Shingu, Wakayama Prefecture, these three buddha-images can be seen enshrined together. The Yakushi Nyorai and Amida Nyorai images were created late in the eleventh century, and the Thousand-Armed Kannon image was created in the fifteenth century.

In Yamagata prefecture, there is a famous mountain range called 'Dewa-Sanzan', the Three Mountains of Dewa, which repeats, in terms of divinities and practices, the pattern of the Shugendo found in Kumano. From this we can see how the prototype of mountain practice from the Kumano region spread across the Japanese archipelago like a kind of blueprint. My family's temple, Koshikidake Kannonji, was one such temple located in Yamgata.

Buddhism is said to have been brought to Mt. Koshikidake by the monk Dosho Shonin in 648. Dosho Shonin (629-700) is an important figure in the history of Japanese Buddhism. He later travelled to Tang China and on his return spread his teachings through Asuka-dera/Hosso-ji Temple and established the Hosso sect. Shugendo is said to have been introduced to the mountain in 874 via Shobo Rigen Daishi, held as the restorer of Shugendo and the founder of the Tozan lineage of Shugendo. At one-point, Kannonji was connected to Mt Yudono, a most secret place and the inner-precinct of the sacred mountains of Dewa.

At the beginning of the seventh century, the political situation in Japan was turbulent and there was no permanent capital. People strongly believed in the spiritual world and held that malevolent forces prevailed from the north-easterly direction (*kimon*, literally "demon gate"). Temples would be placed in this direction to ward off such negative forces. Dosho was sent to find a *kimon* spot for the new capital, then located in the Asuka region in Nara. This was Mount Koshikidake. If you look at a map, you can see that there is a 45-degree line separating Asuka and Mt. Koshikidake. This is the *kimon* direction.

In 1868, the government enacted a series of ordinances requiring the "clarification" of kami and buddha worship, thereby prohibiting any Shinto-Buddhist combination and compromising Shugendo. Contemporary social relationships were greatly impacted, as temples were abolished or converted into shrines. Everything changed, and many statues and documents were destroyed. This marked the end of the combinatory religion that was mainstream until this time.

For this reason, there is a lot of debate in Shugendo, and no lack of objections between priests, practitioners and scholars. To give you an example, more than ten years ago I visited my home temple of Kotakuji at Mt. Haguro. At that time, two scholars were staying there with their students. I thought I'd take the opportunity to get their opinion on the meaning of "Ya-Ho!", a phrase which is shouted by practitioners at the end of a certain part of Haguro's Autumn Peak training. One argued that it had the meaning of "Now we have arrived at the supreme moment" (that is, celebrating the accomplishment). The other scholar disagreed and insisted that it meant "breaking the vicious circle of rebirth in the six realms." The debate got heated and I slipped away quietly without them noticing.

At another time, I was asked to give a lecture on Haguro Shugendo in Tokyo. I was asked about the unique surcoat we wear, which features a checked pattern. I replied that among other things, it represented the sun and moon, that is, Yin and Yang, because that is what I had been taught by my master, Shimazu Kokai, who served as the head of the

Haguro denomination at the time. After my lecture, another priest gave a lecture, and said that the real meaning of the pattern was that it represented Fudo Myo-o's rock-seat. You may know that some Fudo statues have stone pedestals painted with a checked pattern. Those in the hall looked on suspiciously at the differing answers. Anyway, this example may give you some idea that scholars, priests and practitioners may insist on their own interpretations and that the true shape of Shugendo can be elusive.

Shugendo came together on the platform of ancient folk-beliefs related to kami, mountains and ancestors. In Japan's history, mountains were often culturally restricted as the underworld or 'other-worldly', being the haunts of the dead, of wild animals, of ancestors, of the 'undomesticated' elements of society and of awe-inspiring divinity. Shugendo emerged as a broad movement in the seventh century at the crossroads of Buddhist, Daoist and kami-thought, when people began to enter the mountains in an attempt to encounter the experiences of the founding figures of these teachings.

Among these emerged the outstanding figures recognised and revered today among the spiritual ancestors of Shugendo, such as En no Gyoja and Nojosen. This movement has been recognised as Shugendo for around a thousand years, though its reach extends to a vast amount of time beyond that. Throughout the course of history, the cloth of Shugendo was dyed with the colours of esoteric Buddhism, and over time it developed complex rituals centred on death and rebirth in the womb of the mountain.

Shugendo remained influential from the seventh century through to the nineteenth. The *Goma* fires of esoteric practice were once said to have been so popular in the Nara region that they rivalled the light of the rising sun. In the Tokugawa period (1603-1868), when government restrictions led to yamabushi settling permanently in village lodgings, Shugendo's sphere of influence in the community began to grow through the various village-parishes linked to Shugen complexes, and through these parishes the yamabushi madc a strong and lasting impact on the folk practices of the common people. Common rites of passage now referred to as Japanese folk religion were primarily organised and performed by yamabushi. With this shift towards permanent settlement, we find the heart of Shugendo's engagement with popular life, which continues today.

As part of the Meiji Restoration's move towards modernity, Shugendo was vigorously suppressed as a 'backward' cultural tradition. This was the dawn of State Shinto. It is no stretch to say that this process was accompanied by world-shattering violence and was the near deathblow to the beliefs and worldviews of the time. The newly approved version of Shinto was a heavily distorted version of what had previously existed, reconfigured to support a new mythology presented as an unbroken imperial tradition.

Shugendo was outlawed and banned in 1872, being a typical case of the 'mixture' of Buddhism and Shinto. Shugendo shrine-temple complexes were forced to choose between conforming to being either a Shinto shrine or a Buddhist temple, and their practices were banned. One result of the outlawing of Shugendo was that many new religions sprang up to take its place.

Not only Shugendo, but Shinto and Buddhism came under much stricter government control and definition during this period. Independent Shinto shrines were either closed entirely or reconfigured to conform to the new imperialist ideology of State Shinto. Many smaller sects of Buddhism too, like the Fuke sect of Zen, for example, were banned and dismantled. Some sections of Shugendo were able to find relief under the auspices of a sponsoring Tendai or Shingon Buddhist temple, but nonetheless became subject to severe restrictions. This reconfiguration and suppression resulted in a loss of a great deal of knowledge and practice.

DIVINE POWER

為悦衆生故
現無量神力

Where a rainbow appears,
Sunlight follows

In our recent history it has been common to see religious conflict occurring all over the world on an almost daily basis. Though religion is said to exist for human happiness, systematic killings by religious groups continue to happen due to strong beliefs, which deny the recognition of other religious realities. The enemy of their country also becomes an enemy of their god. In some religions, if one fights and dies for their god, it is regarded as a holy death which saves the soul. In Shugendo, divinities never ask us to kill for them. Religions which have many deities are now referred to as polytheistic religions. Among these, we are unable to distinguish true from false, because they are all true. We do not have to argue about it, because they all exist within the same spiritual universe. But sometimes this kind of belief makes us confused as to which deity we should mainly worship. In Shugendo, we have the idea of the fundamental reality of Dainichi Nyorai. This is the Tathagata Mahavairocana, from which all deities can be seen as aspects.

I am talking about religion, but I cannot point out which is the best religion in the world because the states of religion are very diverse. However, I do think there is a connection between religion and war. The teachings of monotheism were spread to the conquered by the victorious. This continual war has also been promoting advancements in technology and science, but we may be in danger as the world seems to be heading in the wrong direction. Shugendo tells us that we had better start thinking about our future in a way of harmony and acceptance.

The origin of Shugendo refers to shamanism in the Eurasian continent, Daoism in China, Buddhism from India and beliefs from Korea. Shugendo was a religion of the common people. All those who wanted to pray to divinities were permitted to worship. This was also reflected in its organisation. In ancient times, yamabushi had no sense of organisational unity. In the Edo period, the authorities made Shugen practitioners join the Honzan or Tozan groups and in the Meiji period, the government ordered them to become subsumed under the Shingon and Tendai sects. The various stages in Shugendo's history as a movement in this sense were shaped by the political manoeuvring of the factions which dominated it. Shugendo, however, had always maintained its obscure status in a good way. Shugendo accepted practitioners without regard for their sect or school. Anybody could practice, even if they were supporters of another temple. Shugendo's approach is like this. Practitioners of Shugendo valued the trust and camaraderie that developed among themselves and had their own sets of beliefs which they prized even more than their own lives.

Before the advent of the Meiji Restoration, the training of Shugenja took on a different appearance when compared to the current forms heavily shaped by esoteric Buddhism. In Komazawa University's Faculty of Buddhism Bulletin, there is a collection of research based on the source materials found in the Naidate Bunko, which were ancient documents transmitted by Hannya-in Temple in Akita Prefecture. These studies tell us about the early Edo period shugenja of the Tohoku region, who, in their travels to the mountains of

Yoshino and Kumano, stopped at various Shugen temples and learned various kinds of teachings and practices. These Tohoku yamabushi would even travel as far at Mt. Hiko in Kyushu. Similarly, in the postscripts found attached to the ancient documents inherited by Koshikidake Kannonji, we find that the successive shugenja periodically left the Dewa region and travelled to places like Kyoto, Nara and Shikoku. In these post-scripts we find that yamabushi were able to travel all over the country spanning periods as long as seven years. In this way, Shugendo supported this kind of practice and its great network acted as a kind of think-tank which enabled practitioners to study and practice broadly and deeply.

As I mentioned earlier, there are mountains all over the Japanese archipelago which enshrine the same three deities as Kumano. Tohoku is no exception, and many 'three-mountain' areas, including Dewa Sanzan, transmit the trinity of Kumano to this day. In fact, this 'three-mountain' schema can be said to have originated from within Kumano, which then spread throughout the land. In line with this theme, in 2006, an exhibition titled "Kumano Faith and Tohoku" was held across the Tohoku Museum of History and the Akita Prefectural Museum. Here, it was made clear that shugenja served as a bridge for Kumano faith and established a unique form of training peculiar to Shugen, the majority of which can now only be understood through the traces left within these ancient documents.

Before the Meiji period, Japan was divided into 68 provinces ruled by feudal lords called *daimyo*. This made it very difficult for people to travel between provinces because they needed special permission to cross any borders. For a period of time, however, itinerant priests like yamabushi were given permission because they had clear reasons to travel for the sake of their practice. My ancestors belonged to the Shugen of Daigoji-Sanboin in Kyoto. They went to Daigoji and Mt Omine to practice and gain priestly and yamabushi qualifications. In total, it must have been a 900 km round trip. On the way there and back they used to stop by various temples of different denominations where they exchanged information as well as teachings and ritual procedures. The old documents of our school describe this kind of collaborative situation. Many of them have postscripts attached outlining where my ancestors went and what they learned. The oldest one belonging to my temple is about 450 years old. This tells us that our Shugendo predecessors had been accumulating knowledge gradually. There was a strong network of yamabushi that supported one another.

The Mandala of the Mountain

In Shugendo, the mountain is a place where the spirits of ancestors and deities gather. The mountain represents the border and barrier between this world and the other. To understand this spiritual world, we have to realise that our senses derive from the material world – our eyes, ears, nose, tongue, body and mind. Through the performance of ceremonies of ritual death and rebirth, a chemical reaction takes place deep within the mountains. Facing ritual death, we start to travel the inner world of the universe. The training of the Ten Realms, Five Stages, Three Crossings and the purification of the six sense roots makes clear the laws of cause and effect. We restrict the freedoms we usually enjoy in our everyday life. Without sleep and through fasting, our casual mindset is stripped little by little and our unconscious mind seeps to the surface. It is under these circumstances that we may become aware of the multitude of phases surrounding nature. The marriage and distinction between divinity and ourselves begins in our mind. This is not just mountain asceticism, but also ritual prayer. Even simple tasks like drawing water or preparing for ceremonies all carry important meanings and we devote ourselves to daily practice in order to realise them. The mountain asceticism of Shugendo is carried out against this kind of backdrop. The mountain sees through us with a severe will.

The consciousness and approach of practitioners is of the upmost importance when considering the concept of 'mountain' in Shugendo. That is, for Shugen, the mountain is not just a geographical location. Rather, the mountain functions as a device which reproduces and gives birth to the secret world of inner-realisation. The practitioner does not even have to set foot in the place. Rather, just by being conscious of this space which we call 'mountain', the practitioner is guided towards wakefulness. This wakefulness cannot be obtained through preliminary training, esoteric Buddhist manners or the performance of ritual-prayer. Rather, the ineffable wakefulness of the universe can only be hinted at and pointed towards. Of course, as practitioners we must enter the peak and undertake practice, however wakefulness entails that our consciousness stretches out to the mandala of the mountain in all moments of our daily-existence.

Prayer and the Human Realm

In Shugendo, the ability to pray and the acts of prayer, confession, praise and gratitude epitomise the experience of the Human Realm; the fifth of the six realms of rebirth. The first time a living being prayed, that must have been the moment it became a human being. It may have been a very simple prayer, for example, mourning a death, the renewal of crops or the healing of disease. Prayer does not have to be complicated. Just serving a cup of tea, arranging flowers, even turning on lights can be a splendid prayer. If we realise that deities exist everywhere, routine duties suddenly turn into noble activities. Our daily life then takes on a new hue, a different quality. It is this kind of casual, everyday life which is important and has the most value in Shugendo. Far from being a symbol of weakness, prayer can be a strong support for people, opening up to a deeper, broader understanding and experience of the world. If we master it, it will be our strongest support. Ritual prayer is just like a pilgrimage to our mind which connects us with the universe. Through ritual-prayer (*kaji-kito*), we will suddenly and steadily have our eyes opened to another kind of existence. Time connects with time when we pray for our future in the past. Our prayer in the present connects with time in the future. This circle of time makes 'no time'. This circle of no existence beyond time makes 'no existence'. We come face to face with notions of reality beyond our thought. The present prayer influences the future or the present occasion. Also, prayer sometimes corrects past events and behaviours. The essence of prayer comes from beyond time and space. To pray now helps us in the future. This is the support for the future from the past. To confess past behaviour influences time and space in the past. The past corrects the present and future and also drives the present.

The primary purpose of Shugendo is not to attain supernatural power, but to study the way of humans and phenomena through facing the myriad buddhas, bodhisattvas and divinities in all things. The real power of these acts is in sharing in the suffering of others. Becoming aware of the existence of deities, we can achieve great peace of mind. The familiar time and space where deities live changes these completely. We come to recognise the circle of time between the past, the present and the future. We can catch time and space beyond our consciousness through prayer and practice. This is the meaning of pursuing prayer.

Once we are able to recognise the existence of deities in nature, we can see the universe beyond time and space in the moments where sunlight shines, in the streaming of water, the waves of the ocean and a gust of wind. This is something beyond conceptual understanding. Nature is healing and provides guidance, giving hope. These things are not in any way special. To find an entrance to this world is the purpose of Shugendo; opening the eyes of wakefulness which will be able to gaze into eternity from the past to the future.

Although many may study profound esoteric manners, none of these things mean anything if the inner spiritual process is not built. There is a spiritual process that needs to be constructed in order to have effect. We have to build up our inner world that way first. This process in the mind is like clockwork. If you do not have it, nothing can be seen in the mind. What one feels depends on this inner process. This is the true meaning and importance behind our practice. It is difficult to talk about Shugendo because it rests on the heart-mind. We go into the mountains and practice various ritual procedures. What practitioners feel depends on their ability to recognise the inner world they have built at that moment. Although practitioners all participate in the same kinds of training, they may experience very different things. The mountain is the stage. What is danced is up to the practitioner. Despite following similar methods, the answers we receive may not be the same.

Kaji-kito - ritual-prayer based on *adhiṣṭhāna* - is not an imaginary world where you escape from reality. The realm of the inner-heart mind, constructed through the observation of the three mysteries, is hyper-dimensional in the sense that it reconstructs the causality (cause-and-effect) of the past, present and future. Practitioners of Shugen establish their methods within the gaps and crevices of time with the will to strongly embody, right down into the deepest layers of our subconscious, the inner world of realisation that has been inherited and diligently transmitted by the predecessors. For esoteric Buddhist monks, the place for *kaji-kito* and the observation of the three-mysteries is found within the space that is the sanctuary of the *goma*-hall. For shugenja, on the other hand, *kito* is not confined to the limits of any kind of space or idea. For yamabushi, shouldering the *Oi* (portable-altar) and carrying the prayers born out of the daily life of the common people was a common thing. Venturing deep into the mountains and secluded valleys, they engaged in purification through ritual death and rebirth, and established a unique methodology of training, exemplified through the practice of *hashiramoto-shinpo*. With this in mind, the inner world of *kaji-kito* is not found somewhere else, but rather is expressed through the real-world itself, just as we experience it, taking place within the real-space of everyday, ordinary life.

Looking to texts such as the 'Chronicles of Yoshitsune', you will find that the yamabushi of old were practitioners of a style of *kaji-kito* which was intimately connected to the daily-lives of the common people. Today, too, practices such as the *furoshiki goma* are still performed in the homes of patron-almsgivers. In the modern period, shugenja were subsumed under the Tendai and Shingon sects and were suppressed in the Meiji period following the Orders to Separate Kami and Buddhas. Practices such as the *furoshiki-goma* and *hashiramoto-shinpo* were thus absorbed into the general curriculum of esotericism and removed from the hands of yamabushi. For this reason, today we find that many yamabushi have become little more than factors within the performance of the *saitō-goma*.

Genkurabe

The bedrock of identity in Shugendo is the participation in annual 'mountain entry' ascetic retreats during which practitioners seclude themselves for a period of time and return to the community with their blessings of spiritual rebirth and renewal. Here too we find the tradition of *genkurabe*; comparing the practitioner's testimony of practice. Some of the more spectacular examples of *genkurabe* include fire walking, competitive ritual ceremonies, sitting in boiling water, rubbing burning torches on the skin and climbing sword-ladders. Shugendo festivals on Mount Togakushi in Nagano, for example, involve the burning of three strands of brushwood affixed to the top of tall pillars. The ashes from these pillars are then used for divination. To highlight another example, I would like to briefly introduce the great yamabushi, Ryuen Honma (1910-1987). Born in Yamagata, he was known as a great master of Shugendo's Dharma-Conch. In 1973, Honma gave a splendid performance as the *sendatsu* responsible for playing the Dharma-conch at the memorial-service organised to mark the 1000th anniversary of Shobo (Rigen Daishi). On camera, Honma was questioned by a reporter from *Chūgai-Nippō* (a religious newspaper based in Kyoto) about the reason for his disregard for the rank of priests in the Daigoji precincts. He shouted, "The ranking of the priesthood was created by a group of people without any merit and if you receive such a thing, you will be punished by the divinities!" leaving everyone around him stunned.

True to his words, which clearly reveal the dignity of a practitioner of Shugen, he lived the life of a true master who turned his back on the high rankings of the priesthood, something which he would have easily been able to obtain if he had so desired. Alongside his outstanding experiential-power and his wonderous ability to bring the Dharma-conch to life in his playing, he has become something of a legend in the Shugen community.

A few years ago, I visited a Buddhist specialty store in Kyoto. When the owner of the store learned that I came from Yamagata, he wanted to share with me his own stories of Master Ryuen Honma. He told the story of when master

Honma came to his store looking to purchase a Dharma-conch. When given one to try, the master's playing made the windowpanes, sliding-doors and sliding screens vibrate, leaving everyone in the store shocked in awe. It was also common for appearances to manifest during his services. Once, after offering salt at the home of a parishioner, a moon appeared in the room and both the salt and the moon vanished together.

神仏一如

Kami and Buddhas
One in Essence.

The Red Mind and the Mirror

The kind of animism expressed within Shinto is the strangest religion because it contains no particular dogma. That does not mean that ancient Shinto is a low-level religion. The teaching of the kami way is to seek and find divinity among the seas, mountains, sun, moon, wind, ebbs and flows. It is a process of feeling, not thinking with the rational mind. An ancient way of saying 'to feel' is *akaki-kokori*, that is, 'red-mind'. Red is the colour of the sun; a divinity which guides our lives. In this sense, 'red-mind' means a clear and cloudless heart in which divinity can be reflected like a mirror.

Ancient peoples obeyed this way of living honestly, but as humans grew wiser this kind of honesty was seen as foolish. As the saying goes, honesty doesn't pay. Through Buddhism, too, the idea of reason within bodhi-wisdom as a cure for ignorance within the mind was introduced. The sun, mountain and ocean gradually diminished as the places of awe they once held. People who approach the sun as a deity are a rarity now. I believe this may be the beginning of humanity's mistake. Let me explain. In ancient Shinto, there are no statues or figures. Instead, there is a mirror. This tells us that to meet with divinities, one has to look into the mirror. Yes, you are part of divine existence. Not only you, but everything which is reflected; humans, animals, trees, grasses, rock and mountains are all deities. Yes, they are all deities.

The mirror is today considered one of the three sacred regalia of Shinto; the mirror, the crescent jewel and the sword. The person who has all three is considered a king. Not the king of the nation, but rather the king of enlightenment. I have already told you the meaning of the mirror. I will tell you the meaning of the other two regalia. The crescent jewel means the imperfect is perfect, which in turn means the mind of awakening must be polished like a jewel. Regarding the sword, it has a double edge. This means that its purpose is to cut away outer obstacles, but more importantly, the obstacles in our mind.

Shugendo had captured localised animism, combined with Shintoism, sucked in Shamanism and Daoism and fused with esoteric Buddhism. In the end, a system of ritual prayer that invokes great power was built up. Yamabushi, through their testimony of practice, were said to hear the voices of divinity in nature, exorcise evil, reveal wisdom and bring in good fortune because they had been practicing asceticism time and time again in deep mountains and valleys. In this way, they directly guided the religious life of people over the centuries.

My family inherited various kinds of procedures which include *norito* (Shinto verses), sutras, mudras, visualisations and mantras. There are ceremonies which are to be performed deep in the mountains and ceremonies which play back the interplay between the celestial plain and the realm of earth. These ritual practices reflect the actual world by shaking the chaos of the universe beyond time and space. In this magnificent dialogue with deities, we visualise their brilliant figures with mantras and mudras like dreaming a dream in the thick darkness of sleep. We face them with space which has no distance, and are fused together, chanting mantras amidst the chaos of the universe.

As I said before, Shinto is a religion which believes that spirit and life reside within everything in the universe. It is the same for the words we speak too. In other words, if one says it will be fine day, it will be fine day. If you say he is OK, he will be OK. In ancient times, people used to feel some holy existence in the words they spoke. That is, that words themselves carried soul and power. This is called *kotodama*, that is, the soul of words. In modern Japan however, this is all but forgotten.

With this in mind, you may be able to understand that *norito*, the verses of Shinto, are considered to carry the essence of *kotodama*. There are various kinds of *norito,* but every single one of them expresses gratitude for all things in the universe with all of one's being. This kind of sincerity is the way of Shinto.

Among the *norito*, the *norito* of purification (*harae no norito*) is a verse which priests regularly chant before the beginning of their ceremonies. This *norito* is based on the mythology surrounding Izanagi and his wife, Izanami. In this story, Izanami dies after giving birth to the fire deity and descends to the depths of the gloomy land of the dead (*yominokuni*). Izanagi, distraught, travels down into the gloomy depths determined to bring her back to the land of the living. When Izanagi finally locates her, he approaches her from behind and yells out for her to return with him. It's too late, however. Izanami turns around and reveals that she is rotting with the signs of decay. Running away, Izanagi is chased by the forces of the dead out to the entrance of the land of the dead, which he then seals with a giant boulder.

Stricken with grief, he plunges himself into a nearby body of water, which cleans away what he had accumulated from travelling to the land of the dead. Many deities were formed from his actions at that time, such as his tears.

This kind of water purification is called *misogi*. When we perform *misogi* while chanting *norito,* it recreates the same conditions that Izanagi experienced, washing away all our *tsumi* and *kegare*, that is, all our pollution and impurities. In Shinto, purification is important because it is said that deities do not approach impurities. Purified, the body becomes a vessel. When we chant *norito*, we can feel the waves of power and the spirits in the words, which reveal our innate wakefulness.

為利邊土衆生

Thus he has come;

To benefit beings across the remotest regions

The patriarch honoured by all practitioners of Shugendo is En no Gyoja. En no Gyoja was a 'flesh and blood' human being. Records state that he was born in 634 and died in 706. After the time of En no Gyoja, mountain-ascetics and priests following in his example continued to enter deep into the mountains with the goal of awakening, which over time developed into Shugendo as a distinct movement. As Shugendo became systematised, so did the vestments, doctrines and implements associated with it. For practitioners of Shugendo, he is considered a second Buddha, like Sakyamuni, and to this day people visit the mountains of Yoshino and Katsuragi where he lived and practiced. En no Gyoja was said to have manipulated the power of ambiguous spirits and was a master of petitionary ritual-prayer. Arrested and sent into exile, he was said to escape every night and fly to Mount Fuji. From this alone you may gather that his existence was considered something beyond ordinary human understanding.

The patriarchs of Shugendo often exhibit a strange appearance. En no Gyoja was said to have horns. Rather than banishing demons, he is said to have taken them on as disciples. Nojosen (the founder revered in Haguro Shugen), was banished due to his non-human appearance and sent away to undertake religious training. When you see the faces of Nojosen and En no Gyoja, you may think that they express severity, blind perseverance or suffering. Although these figures are shown displaying what could be called an ugly, severe appearance, we should not mistake this for common anger or agony. The severity of their expression expresses an atmosphere of power different from common worldliness. In Japan, it is often the case that things which many think should be hidden or shielded from are considered valuable, including things that are ugly, strange or undesirable.

One legend says that En no Gyoja was born gripping a lotus flower. Another states that celestial beings appeared to his mother saying that her son had been 'brought into the world to liberate beings and save the land'. His mother was overwhelmed with fear and abandoned him in the woods on the mountain. Racked with guilt, she travelled back the following day to see if the child had died. She found to her surprise that the boy was happy and was being watched over by a deer and a group of small birds. The harsh rains and lightning of the typhoon did not touch him. Seeing this as fate, she picked him up, caressed him dearly and brought him back home. Whenever En no Gyoja was threatened with danger he was defended by nature.

En no Gyoja was also peculiar as a young boy. He was found writing Brahmic characters, practiced daily in waterfalls, wandered in the mountains and devoted himself to a life of religious practice. There was one priest who accepted En no Gyoja as a disciple. This priest praised his mountain training and instructed him in the ritual procedures of Kujaku Myo-o in order to protect him from demons and harmful spirits in the mountains. En no Gyoja was successful in pacifying demons who were wreaking havoc on the villagers. Moreover, after subduing them, he made them promise to support the Buddhadharma and its practitioners. En no Gyoja practiced across the length and breadth of Japan, celebrating the wisdom and skilful means of the bodhisattvas and buddhas. Eventually, he became an expert practitioner with many spiritual faculties. With his deeds came many admirers. Such achievements also engendered jealous people and enemies.

One story tells us that En no Gyoja was banished to the island of Izu. A jealous high-ranking figure in the government conjured a plot that implicated him in treason. The nefarious trap was so well executed that En no Gyoja was banished to Izu and sentenced to death. On the day of his execution, however, an extraordinary phenomenon occurred. The spirit of the Great Dipper Constellation came down to earth and visited Emperor Monmu, informing him of En no Gyoja's innocence. The incident had been a scheme to disrupt En no Gyoja's influence among the common people and to topple him from the emperor's favour. Vindicated, En no Gyoja returned to his mountain austerities.

En no Gyoja attracted attention as an expert of intercessory incantation and prayer. Modern day people have the choice to look at these legends symbolically or literally. Because of the amazing power of En no Gyoja's prayer, legends arose regarding his supranormal abilities, such as disappearing and flying through the air. To this day, people visit the mountains of Yoshino and Katsuragi, venerated as the birthplaces of Shugendo.

In Shugendo, practitioners take En no Gyoja as their role model. Practitioners enter into the mountains for severe training. This training originates from the tradition that says En no Gyoja was abandoned in the mountain. For the practitioner, this legend implies death and rebirth. The training of the ten realms aims at purification and renewal through the medium of severe training with the aspiration to realise one's buddha nature in this very life. That is, the practitioner experiences death and rebirth through the ten realms in the womb of the mountain.

如風於空中

一切無障礙

Boundless and untouchable
but felt in the quiet of our minds

Japan is known as the land of kami. Shinto, a localised form of faith, evolved and intertwined with the Buddhadharma, which arrived from across the ocean. Here, I will introduce some of the deities most recognised in Shugendo.

Kongo Zao Gongen

The idea that buddhas and bodhisattvas manifest in localised, temporary form is one deeply held in Shugendo. This element of *shinbutsu-shugo* is referred to using the term *gongen*, which means manifestation or avatar, that is, the temporal appearance of a buddha or bodhisattva. Gongen manifest in the myriad forms of nature. In water, they manifest in the form of waves, the tide and sea breeze. On land, they manifest as landscapes and the mountains. In the night sky, they manifest as the moon and stars. The most famous gongen in Shugendo is Kongo Zao Gongen, a manifestation which was realised by En no Gyoja during his ascetic seclusions at Mt Omine. According to legend, En no Gyoja began his ascetic training through practicing the methods of Kujaku-Myo-o. He prayed for the appearance of a figure suitable to liberate beings from suffering in the context of the turbulent period of his time. As a result, various buddhas and bodhisattvas of the past, present and future manifested before him, however they were deemed too gentle and merciful in their appearance. In response, Kongo Zao Gongen broke forth in the form of a wrathful destroyer of demons, depicted with a furious expression, three blazing eyes and bristling hair. In this way, Zao Gongen symbolises the buddhas of the past, present and future, as well as the unity of the mandalas.

There are many legends and folk tales related to Zao Gongen. One story tells of a disbeliever who was carried away by a great eagle only to be placed on the edge of a precipitous cliff. His cries for help were heard by yamabushi who happened to be passing by. They transformed him into a frog, both as a punishment and to allow him to make it down safely. Humbled and desperate to get back to his human form, he made prayers in front of Zao Gongen's image and was immediately transformed.

Another famous gongen is Izuna Gongen, who manifests in the form of a crow-tengu (goblin) riding atop a white fox. This deity is considered a manifestation of Ksitigarbha (Jizo) and Acalanatha (Fudo). Mt. Izuna, which this deity is named after, is located in Nagano. A friend of mine who is associated with the Izuna Shrine in Nagano City told me that there is still a local folk tradition related to Izuna Gongen kept among the members of the shrine association. Here, members take turns caring for images of En no Gyoja and Izuna Gongen for an entire year. The ritual practices associated with them however were unfortunately lost in the Meiji period.

Shogun Jizo

Shogun Jizo is depicted wearing armour riding atop a horse. The term 'shogun' here means 'victorious' and 'Jizo' refers to the bodhisattva Ksitigarbha. In the past, images of Shogun Jizo were often enshrined at sites of Shugen training to encourage practitioners, spurring them on and assisting them with the tenacity and energy of a brave warrior. During the Meiji period, the majority of these images were destroyed. As in other manifestations of Jizo, Shogun Jizo takes on the pain of others as his own and acts as a scapegoat for their suffering. Jizo is popularly depicted helping children suffering at the banks of the Sanzu river (River Styx). There is a theory which says that equestrian people migrated to Japan in ancient times. Conquering the local agricultural people, they established a dynasty which remains with us to this day. Shogun Jizo's features may hold memories which reach back to these ancient times, symbolising the intertwining of these two ways of life.

Jubutsu

Jubutsu are a presence carried forward from ancient times. These are stones or statues usually found enshrined at the entrance to a home or village, or at the border between lands. They are also referred to as *Dosojin* which means 'divine ancestor enshrined beside the road'. This term however does not express their full function.

Jubutsu means a 'cursing object', and specifically an object which curses and wards off evil. Drawing in good luck, they act as a barrier to prevent evil from entering the village or home. There are jubutsu which have been in the same places for countless generations. Here, some of them still remain the object of worship and veneration. The jubutsu in the photograph on the previous page is located in Sagae city, in Yamagata Prefecture. It is known locally as the *Sai-no-kami* and represents the female reproductive organ. People pray to the Sai-no-kami in the hopes that they will be blessed with a child quickly and easily. Due to the conservative nature of modern sensibilities, jubutsu have in some cases become an object of embarrassment. Also pictured is another jubutsu which was enshrined at Mt Koshikidake for two millennia. There are nine holes in it, representing the nine celestial bodies. Here, the jubutsu tells us something of the background and origin of Shugendo.

Fudo Myo-o (Acalanatha Vidyaraja)

Fudo Myo-o is well known across the world of Buddhism. The stone platform he sits upon represents his immovable determination. In his right hand he holds a vajra-sword which symbolises the wisdom and skilful means to destroy

the kleshas. In his left hand he holds a coiled rope symbolising both the compassion he extends to all those who are suffering as well as the binding of demons. His eyes look up and down, symbolising the bodhisattva path. His fangs protrude upwards and downwards intimidating evil in every direction.

He is a wrathful manifestation of Mahavairocana, guiding even the most stubborn beings towards wakefulness. Fudo Myo-o is portrayed as a terrifying deity, however his head and body are shaped like that of an infant. His character and personality is said to extend back to the slave class of ancient India. In this way, he reveals his duty as a servant. Due to his innocence, he is said to sometimes grant unfulfilled wishes. Another form of Fudo is Kurikara, which, in the form of Fudo's attributes of rope and sword, appears as a dragon coiled around a vajra-sword. Fudo Myo-o's attributes reveal the innate suchness of the ten realms, which expresses the wakefulness of perfect Buddhahood.

Kujaku Myo-o (Mahamayuri Vidyaraja)

Unique among the *vidyaraja*, Kujaku Myo-o possesses a calm elegance and dignity as opposed to the wrathful rage of the others. The peacock which Kujaku myo-o rides upon is said to be the enemy of snakes and immune to their venom. In this way, Kujaku Myo-o provides antidotes to counteract the poisons of the evil passions of sentient beings just like a peacock which is able to eat poisonous weeds and harmful insects without injury. Kujaku Myo-o also holds a central place in Shugendo and in the legends of En no Gyoja.

Kanzeon Bosatsu (Avalokitesvara Bodhisattva)

Kanzeon's name means to perceive (hear) the sounds of the world. In this way the various forms of Kanzeon symbolise the skilful means which compassionately nourish the bodhicitta of beings to fruition, and which assists beings according to their specific ailments, inclinations and dispositions. This is the meaning of Kanzeon's depiction, which shows one hand with a lotus bud and the other hand guiding it to flower. Sho-Kanzeon (Arya-Avalokitesvara) may appear in any number of thirty-three forms in order to offer assistance and guide beings. Among these, the form of with eleven faces is well known. These faces depict the various human emotions. There is a secret face on the back which is often misinterpreted as having a jovial expression. However, it is better understood as one of extreme and insane anger. This form of Kanzeon is thus also honoured as a deity of protection who acts as a strong shield against evil.

Sanbo Dai-Kojin

Kojin refers to a class of unbridled, wild divinity. Traditionally the spirits of disaster, calamity, obstacle, war, and so on, were all collectively referred to as *kojin* or *ara-mitama* ('rough spirits'). These unbridled spirits were enshrined and honoured with the aim of harmonising them. From this, you may gather that kami carry an ambiguous nature, capable of both blessing and curse. Sanbo Dai-Kojin is popularly known in folk-religion as a deity of the hearth and therefore associated with the modern-day kitchen. However, this image is due to the deity being the personification of fierce wilderness and the unpredictable power of nature. The term *sanbo* usually refers to the three treasures of the Buddha, Dharma and Sangha. Here, however, it refers to the three poisons of ignorance, aversion and craving. Kojin is enshrined and honoured to avoid obstacles related to the three poisons. Kojin is also known as a 'placenta deity' and plays a key role in Shugendo's embryological discourse.

Tengu

Though the origin of the Tengu lies in the Garuda of India and the celestial-phantoms of China, the quintessential Tengu figure with its long nose or beak and wings is very familiar in Japan as a symbol of divinity. This Tengu also has a long background in the world of Shugendo.

You may know about *torii*, the large gates found at Shinto shrines. The torii is actually a big perch for birds. In ancient times, birds (particularly the crow) were considered to be messengers of the gods or used by the spirits of the deceased to come and go between one world and the other. Some of the earliest excavated articles from Jomon and Yayoi period ruins (around 14000 BC to 300 AD) feature bird motifs. Across Asia and especially in Tibetan Buddhism birds are associated with funeral ceremonies where the body is offered to birds. As a matter of fact, birds and their link to the dead may be a common religious element around the world.

Deep in the mountains in places associated with Shugendo, Tengu are said to live and serve as the divinities of sacred places. Among these are Tengu such as 'Tarabo' of Mt. Atago, 'Jirobo' of Mt. Hira, 'Sanjakubo' of Mt. Akiba, and 'Sankobo' of Mt. Haguro. Legends of Tengu speak of the deep relationship between ancient people and mountains. A classic example of the Tengu featured in combinatory form is the deity Izuna Gongen. This deity is wrapped in white snakes, rides on a white fox, has a lingam nose or beak, wings, and is engulfed in a flame-nimbus. The lingam is a symbol of nature, the fox is a symbol of good harvest (because of its childbearing), the snakes allude to Benzaiten and the kleshas, the fox to Dakini-ten and the bird nimbus flame to Fudo-myo-o and Garuda.

The Tengu in this sense can also be seen as a manifestation of these deities. You may get an idea from this about how the Tengu is an original character of Shugendo which lets us realise the existence of deities through nature. While the Tengu has this divine nature, on the other hand to 'become a Tengu' means to become excessively boastful and to succumb to conceit. It is said that if you rely on Dharma-power to fulfil your own ruthless or greedy desires, or if your practice leads to greater pride, honour or obsession with position, or if you attempt to indulge in teachings and practices without guidance or proper empowerment, you will fall into the Way of the Tengu. Folklore tells us that the priest-turned-Tengu is caught in the purgatory of the Tengu World; kept out of the hell realms due to its study of Buddhism but also kept out of the Heavenly realms due to its conceit. The combination of Buddhist wisdom with its misuse and lack of appropriate aspiration leaves the Tengu outside of the three lower realms, but nonetheless beyond the realm of humans. The Tengu in this way teaches practitioners to break the pride and conceit in their hearts. These everyday appearances of the Tengu in folklore and popular culture speak to the way people have held them in awe.

我今見聞得受持

Now,
beholding the Buddha with the eyes
and hearing truth with the ears,
I will endeavour to receive and maintain it

Shugen doctrine ultimately takes form through practice, both through mountain-entry asceticism and through its unique ritual-sadhana. Just as the *kasaya* in Buddhism signifies the refuge of the practitioner, the implements and vestments of the practitioner of Shugen all serve as devices which simultaneously guide doctrinal-osmosis and reflect the cultivation and inner-realisation of the practitioner. I will now introduce some of the implements and practice-items used in Shugendo, along with their basic doctrinal significance.

Tokin

There are various kinds of hood, or tokin, in Shugendo. The most common is a small cap worn on the forehead which symbolises Mahavairocana's crown of five-wisdoms and the armour of a bodhisattva; one who gives benefit to all beings. The twelve folds of the tokin reveal the twelve links of co-dependent-arising and the black colour represents their root: ignorance. Further, the six grooves on the left symbolise the endless cycle of samsara amidst the six realms of Buddhist cosmology. The six grooves on the right symbolise the six ways of assisting beings in the six realms.

Yuikesa

The yuikesa is a folded Buddhist surplice with six dharma-wheels or tufts. Generally speaking, they are worn with four on the front and two on the back, symbolising the practice of the six paramitas. The original vestment of Shugendo was a very simple nine strip Buddhist surplice which was folded for ease of practice in the mountains. These nine folds along with the practitioner symbolises the wondrous principle of the innate suchness of the ten realms, and its overall shape symbolises the perfect harmony of the three-fold body of the Tathagata. The features of the yuigesa, depending on the sect, can reveal the practitioner's rank and denomination. There is a legend which says that the yuikesa dates back to the time of En no Gyoja. Here, a monkey is said to have picked up En no Gyoja's ragged Buddhist robe and restored it to use by folding and tying it around his neck with a rope.

Suzukake

Suzukake refers to the standard hemp vestments of Shugendo which are used in the mountains. The outer and bottom sections together represent the mandalic view of the universe. The outer section is made of nine pieces, expressing the nine sections of the Vajradhatu mandala. The bottom section is made up of eight pieces representing the eight-petalled lotus flower at the centre of the Womb mandala. The three folds on the back represent the three poisons of attachment, aversion and ignorance. The six folds on the front represent the six paramitas, which constitute the practice of a bodhisattva. In this way, practitioners practice the six paramitas while carrying the three poisons.

Kaino-o

The kaino-o refers to the two lengths of rope worn around the waist, however traditionally it referred to the rope attached to the Dharma-conch. In addition to their practical use in the mountains, both ropes carry layers of meaning, ultimately expressing the non-separation of the Vajra and Womb mandalas.

Hisshiki

The hisshiki is an animal-pelt worn on the waist of the practitioner to be used in the mountains as a seat. Regardless of the material, it symbolises the pelt of a lion; a reference to the mount of the bodhisattva Manjusri. In this sense it represents ferocious effort and exertion towards transforming fundamental ignorance through mountain training.

Kyahan

The kyahan are a pair of cloth coverings worn to protect the legs during mountain-training. Their shape, colour and the way they are tied also carry layers of meaning. The ties at the top and bottom symbolise the way of the bodhisattva, which is 'aspiring to bodhi above; liberating beings below'.

Shakujo

In Shugendo, sound plays a very important role. The sounds of various implements have the ability to cut off the illusions held by the six sense organs and the interruption of meditative absorption by discontinuous sound is an aspect of Shugendo ritual. The Shakujo is a metallic cane with rings threaded through it. In Shugendo, the most common number used is six, symbolising the six paramitas. The ornamental-head of the Shakujo has various features which symbolise the fundamental equality between beings and buddhas. Shaking the Shakujo, practitioners become conscious of transforming the suffering of the six paths of rebirth. The sound carries the meaning of waking beings from the slumber of the six realms of samsara.

Juzu

Juzu are prayer-beads. The general purpose of the juzu is to break the kleshas and, through cultivation, to purify them as the fruit of the Buddha's wisdom. Various kinds of juzu are used depending on the denomination. The juzu of Shugendo are characterised by the sharp abacus-shape of the beads, which symbolise the sword of Fudo-Myo-o.

Horagai

Horagai means 'Dharma-conch'. The horagai is used to mark important points in Shugendo's mountain-entry asceticism, for example the beginning of liturgies, ceremonial cues and so on. The various scores of the horagai also express different teachings. The sound of the horagai is likened to the inner realisation of the preaching of the Tathagata and for this reason it is compared to a lion's roar. Just as a lion's roar causes other animals to tremble and prepare for death, the Tathagata's sermon immediately dispels the afflictions of beings, leading them to the realm of awakening.

Oi

Yamabushi carry a portable altar called an Oi on their backs to store ritual implements during mountain pilgrimage. The Oi serves both symbolic and practical functions and is constructed in a way so as to reflect the Buddhist worldview of Shugendo. During mountain training, the Oi becomes a womb and reflects concepts of death and rebirth. As with the Womb mandala, the essence and characteristics of the Oi are likened to a mother's compassion. As the focal point of mountain training's embryological discourse, the Oi acts as the principal image during ceremonies.

Kongozue

The Kongozue ('Vajra-cane') is a walking-stick used in the mountains. Its purpose is to support the practitioner. Traditionally, the kongozue acts as both a stupa and a grave-marker.
Depending on the grade of the practitioner, various kinds of kongozue are used.

Pure Mind – like morning dew on leaves.
Hard to keep, but unforgettable.

Shugendo is a religion that originated from the mountains. All meaning comes from the land, that is, nature. This is why mountains and valleys have been the basis of Shugendo's guiding beliefs since ancient times. In the mountain beliefs of Shugendo, the mountains are venerated as the dwelling of ancestors and kami. The natural world is seen to act as a border and barrier to another world.

What is unique about Shugendo is the combination of Buddhist cosmology and what can be called localised kami-beliefs. *Jukkai-shugyo*, the ten realms training in the mountain, is a series of initiations which take away the casual freedoms of daily life, revealing the conditions of cause and effect. Going without sleep and fasting, practitioners lose all feeling in their bodies, but are filled up with a new recognition and awareness. Under these conditions, they also become aware of the unseen phases of nature. Here, in their mind, the marriage between divinity and themselves and the dance of all creation begins. This is why practitioners of Shugendo are called yamabushi; someone who submits to the mountain.

The six realms of rebirth, from the hells to the celestial realm, are referred to as *rokkon*; the six realms of rebirth which constitute the realm of delusion or samsara. People wander over and over through these six realms in bewilderment, unable to find their way. The remaining four realms, from the Sravaka to the Buddha, are the realms of awakening. In Shugendo, practitioners enter all ten realms ritually, amidst the chemistry of the mountain. Once, there were mountain ranges all over Japan where Shugendo was practiced. The best-known of these today is the Omine range, which extends across Nara and Mie Prefectures. At Omine pilgrims travel along a 150km rugged mountain path, along which there are 75 places of worship called *nabiki*. Practitioners take around a week to travel along this path, stopping to pray and undergo initiations along the way. The traditions of Omine have retained some old customs, however today the Ten Realms practice is not really pursued there. The only place where this tradition is really kept alive is Dewa Sanzan— the Three Mountains of Dewa, but as it is forbidden to talk about it, I cannot talk about it either.

I participated in the mountain training organized by Kotakuji Shozen'in temple at Mt. Haguro, one of the Three Mountains of Dewa, for over two decades before reviving my family temple. I inherited the teachings and practices of Haguro from Reverend Shimazu Kokai, head priest of Haguro Shugendo, and was permitted to transmit these ritual-teachings. However, the geography of Mt. Haguro is very different from that of Mt. Koshikidake. This being the case, the training is adjusted, reflecting the unique schedule of ceremonies as revealed by the landscape itself. I would like to make it clear that even if I reveal aspects of our Koshikidake style of Ten Realms training, it does not mean that I am revealing the style of the mountain training secret to Haguro.

Shugendo is a bodhisattva practice where lay people aspire to hone their bodies and minds and to awaken to the ultimate reality of the Buddha through the dignity of daily life. By undertaking the asceticism of the mountain-peak, practitioners reveal their fundamental buddha-nature. In the mandala of the mountain, one is wrapped up in the world of the Buddha just as a child is formed in a mother's womb. Those desperately searching for their nature will find through the womb of the mountain that this nature exists nowhere else but in their own heart-mind.

As mentioned, the most well-known mountain training of Shugendo is the training which occurs along the Omine mountain range, called *okugake*, starting from Yoshino in Nara Prefecture to Kumano Hongu Taisha in Mie Prefecture. This pilgrimage path follows the paths set by En no Gyoja, and to this day it remains famous as the hardest training in Shugendo. Omine is a sacred site for my family because my ancestors visited there. An Omine yamabushi who is a friend of mine told me that during the *okugake* training there are very few places where one can find water. To travel deeply into the mountains carrying everything one needs is a remarkable effort. My friend also told me that it is not uncommon for people to go missing.

On the Kumano side of the pilgrimage trail there are three major shrines: Kumano Hongu Taisha, Kumano Hayatama Taisha and Kumano Nachi Taisha. Together, they are referred to as Kumano Sanzan. These "three mountains of Kumano" have been a focal point of worship stemming back to ancient times, predating even En no Gyoja. As Buddhism became established from around the ninth century, a unique discourse now referred to as *honji-suijaku* (literally, "original ground and traces") grew. This is the idea that local kami (deities) were in actual fact manifestations of a buddha.

According to this idea, people venerated the local deity of Kumano Hongu Taisha as the Buddha Amida, the deity of Kumano Hayatama Taisha as the medicine Buddha Yakushi Nyorai, and the deity of Kumano Nachi Taisha as Senju-Kannon; the Thousand-Armed Avalokitesvara. Going right back to ancient times, pilgrims visited Kumano as a Pure Land populated by divinities, bodhisattvas and buddhas. As Kumano is relatively close to the old capital of Kyoto, it became a popular site of pilgrimage visited not only by common people but also by emperors and the nobility. The spectacle of the many pilgrims advancing towards Kumano like a procession of ants led to the expression *ari-no-kumano-mode* (*ari* is "ant"). Popular belief held that Yakushi Nyorai healed the sick, Kannon promised happiness in this world and Amida guided one after death. It is quite natural that people want to live happily and healthily and wish for a peaceful death. This idea fused with beliefs related to the veneration of mountains, and thus deities were enshrined at mountain sites all across Japan.

The blueprint for worship established at Kumano soon spread to other areas of Japan. In the Tohoku region, where I live, Dewa Sanzan became another famous sacred site of Shugendo. Mirroring Omine, Dewa Sanzan had Amida enshrined at Mt. Gassan, Sho-Kannon (Arya-Avalokitevara) at Mt. Haguro and Dainichi Nyorai (Mahavairocana) at Mt. Yudono. These three were also enshrined at Mt. Koshikidake, which attracted many pilgrims. Performing religious ceremonies and services to the spirits of ancestors in the mountains is an ancient custom in Japan. In Shugendo, returning to the mountain means to die. It is natural to say our death is a departure from life to the other world. That gate is the mountain.

We cannot pass through this gate with our casual, everyday bodies and minds. Just as our everyday lives and surroundings are connected to mountains, so is life connected to death. From this you may understand that in Shugendo, the mountain is a system which lets us experience ritual death and rebirth. This ritual death through the ten realms practice is a secret ceremony for rebirth. Gestating our inner world within the mountains, it becomes our outer world.

The mountain complex is a gate to both the celestial plane and the underworld, as well as being the territory of divinities. Making a pilgrimage through the ten realms, we also develop a relationship with divinities. Once we enter the mountain, our ordinary life vanishes. The mountain's peak is the critical point between Earth and Heaven. Here is the lotus-flower seat where the deities descend. Whether this world can be realized or not depends on the practitioner.

Sleepless and without food, practitioners continually offer ritual services dimly lit by candlelight. Elsewhere, family and friends may be enjoying a delicious meal in the comfort of their home and sleeping pleasantly. To them, the ten realms practice might be seen as a foolish, meaningless endeavour. Returning home, we might be scoffed at with no praise for participating in such a thing. Shugendo originally was without big temples and large numbers of believers. Following in the footsteps of hermits, ritual prayer is thus undertaken without any profit amidst the human realm. In the mountain, however, we are treated to the greatest temple, with every plant, gust of wind, star and the darkness of night as our deities. Through the process of ritual death and rebirth, practitioners come to awaken to true reality and existence, embodying the ultimate truth of the universe.

There is no pleasure in mountain training. Fasting and sleeplessness bring the kleshas – habitual afflictions and reactive patterns – bubbling to the surface. Practitioners are bothered by these from beginning to end. The three poisons of ignorance, craving and aversion, along with desire for fame, vanity, conceit and so on, gradually screen out potential practitioners. That may be a good result for them. It's one of the possible answers which may be realised through ritual practice. That is, mountain-training reveals what is truly important to us.

If there is a hell, go there. When in the realm of hungry spirits, go hungry. In the realm of animals, act on your instincts. In the realm of the ashura, fight. In the human realm, be tormented by the markers of existence. In the heavenly realm, gloat with pride and arrogance. In the mountain, many questions are repeated in the mind and practitioners expose everything to the divinities of the mountain. One meets with both sagehood and devildom, and realises what it is to live. The mountain is such a place.

In Shugendo we find that doctrinal stances are summarised by idioms such as '*the mutual-interpenetration of the ten realms*', '*the three-thousand aspects in a single moment*', '*the mind itself as fundamentally endowed with the ten realms,' 'the mind as suddenly vajra', 'the nonduality between ignorance and sagehood'*, and so on. This tells us that a single moment is replete with the ten realms, as well as the wakefulness and delusion within it.

The mountain-asceticism of the ten realms encompasses every realm which exists in the minds of each and every being, from hell to the realm of Buddhahood. The ten realms of Buddhist cosmology include the fearful realm of the hells, the desperation of the realm of hungry ghosts, the fear and instinctive behaviour of the animal world, the jealousy of the warring spirits (ashuras), human attachment and gratitude, God-like arrogance, the learning of the sravaka-buddhas, the realisation of the pratyeka-buddhas, bodhisattvahood and buddhahood. Mandalas are naturally revealed by the mountain and thus the training depends on the layout of the landscape and its topography.

Ten Realms mountain-asceticism is also referred to as 'the practice of moss,' as practitioners are forbidden to wash their faces, bathe or brush their teeth. Climbing on all fours, they enter the animal realm. Fasting contributes to the practice of the realm of the hungry ghost. The contents of the practices associated with the ten realms are not explained one by one. Each event takes place at the sound of the horagai (Dharma-conch) and it's uncertain when exactly the sound will ring out. As fatigue increases due to lack of sleep, the flow of time begins to warp as if it were a living creature. A short moment can seem like an eternity, long moments can seem instantaneous; the flow of time during the mountain-entry retreat is never uniform. The mountain training held at Mt. Haguro takes nine days to complete. At Mt. Koshikidake, it is shortened even further. This being the case, ritual ceremonies are performed almost constantly, so practitioners have almost no rest. They enter into an intense and demanding situation, physically and mentally, losing all sense of time, and finally are only able to say whether it is day or night.

In summary, the practice of the Ten Realms is the realisation in one's own heart of the mutual interpenetration of the ten realms. There are many secret aspects to this practice, but I'd like to introduce a few details concerning mountain training as it is practiced at Mt. Koshikidake. Not all practices are included. For example, hunger is not really experienced because it takes time to really starve. An understanding of this realm, however, is developed through the experience of fasting.

In Shugendo, the ritual to enter the mountain is very important in signifying the border between our everyday lives and the other world. We have to make certain that we make this deep shift in order to experience this world through the mountain. At first, our names are called as Shugendo practitioners in front of the torii gate, and we are purified at the Yamanokami (mountain deity) shrine using an old Shinto ritual and a unique Shugendo implement called a Bonten. After this, we ask permission to enter the mountain from the mountain-deity and swear that we will not commit any kind of bad behaviour. Inside the shrine of the mountain deity, it is possible to understand the generous character of traditional Japanese animism. At the altar of the mountain peak (*minegyo-saidan*) you can also see the combinatory nature of Shugendo.

In mountain training, it is very important to put an end to our casual life. We have to be conscious about the meaning of mountain training. Because of that, we wear yamabushi vestments which are layered in symbols, purify ourselves, and receive permission to enter the mountain from the deities. "Yamabushi" means "to submit to the mountains." Practitioners must strike a bell and swear an oath before they depart.

Mt. Koshikidake is a popular hiking spot, but we must recognise that we are entering the mountain which functions as a stage for the purpose of religious training. We are entering the mountain to experience an understanding of the essence of the ten realms. To enter this spiritual phase, we symbolically perform a funeral-banquet for ourselves, experience death and make a break with our bodies. We draw water for ourselves for the last time at the Fourth Bridge before embarking on a funeral procession towards the 'other world' which will connect us with the ten realms.

In Japanese, the number four is pronounced "*shi*", which is the same pronunciation as the word "death". The significance of the fourth bridge lies in the fact that it reminds us to be conscious of the image of death. Once we cross the fourth bridge, the ritual of rebirth begins. We then approach the entrance of the mountain trail without speaking as a sign that we have lost our bodies. The silent parade makes us remember that we are in the infernal regions. Although later we will experience the pain of acrid smoke as part of the Hell Realm practice, in this moment we are conscious of the procession from Paradise towards Hell.

There are ten slopes, large and small, shaped like a dragon clinging to a sword. Although these ten slopes do not correspond to the ten realms, they remain very important in letting us dedicate ourselves to the mountain pilgrimage. They allow us to see the mountain as divine territory and experience a spiritual shift. We receive a special purification rite at the border crossing between the two worlds and continue on into the tabooed land.

Just beyond this trail, there is a secret place where we will undergo waterfall ascetic training later. We receive the power of the sacred water by chanting the Sutra of water. This ritual, which involves purification by sacred water, also corresponds to a portion of the daily liturgies we perform.

The fourth slope is the most demanding point of the journey. We crawl up the difficult landscape on all fours like animals striving to reach the top first. This is the animal realm of immediacy, instinct and brutality. It is difficult to realize these ideas on an intellectual level, but if we cultivate the correct mindset and have our inner worlds connect to the universe, these practices will act to awaken us. Once we have accomplished mountain training, we can recall the entire process by memory and recitation to continually sharpen ourselves.

We arrive at the edge of Mt. Tsugayama, where we can rest for a while. But here we are on the cusp of the six realms of desire, the 'fire break' area. For this reason, we have to purify that which we carry over from our everyday lives.

Here, we chant a Sutra dedicated to Fudo Myo-o because Fudo, as an embodiment of all ten realms, acts as a judge. We pray to Fudo to receive protection and escape from the six realms of samsara.

Fudo Myo-o (Acalanatha Vidyaraja) is one of the most popular figures in Japan due to his impressive appearance. As mentioned, he is an aspect of Dainichi Nyorai (Mahavairocana). Some may think that he is some kind of warrior god because of the big sword in his hand and his wrathful appearance. However, this sword is not a weapon, but rather a Buddhist implement to drive away the kleshas.

I want you to look closely at his appearance. His head is large and disproportionate to his small body. His body is short and stocky like that of a child. Fudo Myo-o's hair is modelled on the style of the servant-slave class found in ancient India. His basic character is that of a devoted servant to the Buddha.

Each element of his appearance carries layers of meaning, just as his sword does. To put it simply, the wrinkles in the middle of his forehead express his mercy and compassion towards the agony of the world's people. He squints horribly with his eyes facing different directions, but this symbolises his far-reaching gaze. He bares his canine teeth which point

up and down, showing his mind of wakefulness (*bodhicitta*) and compassionate action. The rope he is holding is to bind evil and rescue beings, relieving those bound with suffering. The nimbus-flame he shoulders is in the shape of a firebird of legend that eats up the three poisons.

His skin is often shown as the colour of mud, symbolising the mud of drowning amidst samsara. His body is covered with mud because he has dived into the pond of samsara. It symbolises his mind to save those in agony and hopeless grief. Fudo Myo-o is a deity who has great mercy behind his horrible appearance. This scary appearance guides those who cannot be awakened by teachings alone.

Let me speak more about Fudo Myo-o from another point of view. In the giant universe of folk and Buddhist cosmology there is a group of famous deities called Ju-o ("ten kings") who are regarded as the ten judges of hell. They are held to be awesome existences because they preside over the weighing of karma belonging to the dead person. The first judge of the dead is called Shinko-o and is considered to be an avatar of Fudo Myo-o. He determines the destiny of the dead. This means that Fudo Myo-o can manage our lives even after death.

On this occasion I would like to explain my point of view concerning the connection between Buddhism and other religions. First, I have to tell you about the concept of *Chu*, or the intermediate state. It is a period of grief and mourning in Buddhism which lasts seven weeks. Folk-tradition tells us that the dead must appear before a different judge every week. Seven judges administer justice during this period. After the *Chu* period, the 3rd, 7th and 33rd anniversaries will continue on as important days. This is the reason ten judges in total are needed.

These ten deities did not exist in early Buddhism but are deities which are associated with the Ten Kings of Hell in ancient Manicheanism, founded in Iran in the 3rd century. I have been thinking that the ten judges in Manicheanism and the Sabbath (which occurs every seven days in Christianity) were combined along the Silk Road to form the concept of *Chu*. These combined under the influence of Chinese thought to produce the veneration of the Ten Kings in 10th Century China. One of the deities, Taizan-O, for example who is the 7th judge of the Juo, is a Chinese deity.

Continuing on with the ten realms, in the realm of Humanity we practice ritual confession, an action which is said to be unique to humans. We climb upwards chanting the mountain *nenbutsu* to cleanse our six sense roots. There is a procedure for confessing our transgressions at the beginning of our prayers. We cannot praise the deities unless we practice confession. It is the same process in the mountains except we are not seated. This concludes the preparation for prayer.

At the next stage we experience awe at the wide field of vision near the peak of the mountain. Here is the heavenly realm. This realm, however, is still part of the six realms of suffering. To escape this vicious cycle, we reaffirm our aspiration to Buddhahood and strike a bell. We hit the bell firmly and escape from the vicious cycle of the six realms of desire.

We continue onwards from the six realms of samsara to the four noble realms, crossing from Mt. Tsugayama to Mt. Koshikidake. The trail goes through the pocket between the two mountains and evokes the feeling of falling into a bottomless pit. We continue to crawl ahead chanting the Mantra of Light for the spirits of the dead.

The Realm of the Sravakabuddha involves performing a ritual at a sacred site of chestnut trees. The ruins here mark the site where the old Kannonji temple once stood. We offer incense to the lineage of successive head priests and deities existing in the mountain. Though it looks like we are close to the peak of the mountain, there remains a long, tough trail ahead. This symbolically connects us to the Realm of Learning (Śrāvaka). While we are in the four noble realms, there still remains the risk of acting hastily in a gratified or self-satisfied manner. Many practitioners fall into evil courses because of their self-complacency, and we should be mindful that the demons of conceit always lie in wait to deceive us. For this reason, we pray for the protection of deities in order to accomplish our vows and mountain training safely.

We arrive at a sacred site where an old pine tree stands. This is regarded as a holy existence of Mt. Koshikidake. We can relate to the deities at this site. To connect with the deities, we have to recognise the existence of beings beyond humans and other species. We chant 'The Verse of Original Enlightenment' accordingly. The summit of Mt. Koshikidake is near, but still feels so far away to us.

We chant the sutras related to the six paramitas of a bodhisattva; the six practices of giving, moral-discipline, patience, effort, meditation, and wisdom. These practices reveal to us the mind of the bodhisattva. We are determined to devote ourselves to the relief of all beings as we look out over the city where people live. We must etch that in our heart forever, because this is the noblest aim of our practice.

What we realize through mountain training is that all aspects of creation are parts of the universe, which is the world of Buddha. The ten steps from hell to Buddha all belong to this world. If there is a hell we must go there, we must confess our transgressions and give thanks in the world of the human and be elegant in the world of devas. We should accept everything and go through all processes towards Buddhahood with the response, 'Uketamau!' ("I accept!"). At the peak of the mountain, we chant a sutra dedicated to Avalokitesvara and make an oath to take away the sufferings which other beings experience.

There are many other important events, secret rites, rituals and layers of interpretation, but I hope this gives you some idea of what is involved in the Mountain Entry Practice of Shugendo. The world in which humans live is forever plagued by hardship and worries. We have to understand and feel others' pain or distress as our own agony. We cannot assist people without knowing them. To realise the virtue of common everyday life during this period of strenuous practice is one of the most important purposes of the mountain training.

Valley training

Rain, wind, snow
Floating across the earth
Forever to remain

There are two kinds of ascetic training at Mt. Koshikidake, corresponding to the Womb and Vajra mandalas. The first is 'mountain training' (峰行; *minegyo*), the trails of which are also shared by hikers. The second is 'valley training' (澤行; *sawagyo*). Unlike mountain training, valley training occurs deep in the mountain in a sheltered and secluded place. It is not easily accessible. During valley training, practitioners walk in between steep ridgelines which envelope them like a curtain. The water of the valley symbolises the bloodline of our lineage. In short, practitioners carry out their training and ceremonies with a keen awareness of what they have inherited from the ancestors of the practice. As the practitioners continue on deeper into the valley, they are quickly cut off from where the previous ritual-ceremony occurred. In such a situation, the passage of time begins to warp, one's memory plays tricks and one becomes confused as to how far one has actually travelled. In the chaos of this state of consciousness, practitioners brush up their minds and spirits.

According to the doctrines of Shugendo, beings are naturally pure, just as they are. While in the mother's womb, the body begins to form. The mind of bodhicitta and the kleshas arise simultaneously. In this sense, the valley is taken as the womb itself. In the chaos of the unique swampy terrain of the valley, practitioners practice to reveal the truth of this innate purity, which is the perspective of a buddha. In this way, valley training repeats the ten realms practice of mountain training.

I will now outline some of the processes which make up valley training.

First, practitioners arrive at the shrine of the mountain deity and petition to be able to enter the valley. As a mark of their oath to leave their everyday lives behind, practitioners hit a small bell. The sendatsu (ritual leader) announces the beginning of valley training and sets the stage for practice.

Ozawa-kudari

Ozawa-kudari means to descend into Yomi, that is, the underworld. Abandoning any lingering affection for their everyday lives, practitioners make the descent. As the Dharma-conch echoes through the valley, they mourn their situation and arrive at a riverbank called Toritsuki. This becomes the Sanzu River, which is similar in concept to the river Styx. The pilgrimage transforms into a funeral procession.

Oshimefuchi

From the Sanzu River, practitioners continue on down steep slopes leading to an abyss. Here, a ceremony takes place at the site known as Oshimefuchi. Part of the ceremony involves a practitioner taking the Dharma-bow and shooting an arrow. Like the kami-body of Mt. Yudono, Oshimefuchi symbolises the female genitals. The act of shooting the arrow implies conception. That is, the practitioner receives new life and scrambles up the stream. This is the beginning of ritual death and rebirth.

Kurikara

At a small pond known as Nata-Otoshi, practitioners perform ablutions before continuing on to Otsubo, where they perform *misogi* water purification. Like animals, they use all their limbs to climb up the steep rock formation known as Kurikara. Here, they see their hunger-stricken faces reflected in the water and enter the realm of the violent Ashura. In this way, practitioners travel through the realms of the hells, hungry ghosts, animals and ashura.

Gyoja-Gaeshi

While chanting the mindful recitation of confession, practitioners climb the rock known as Gyoja-Gaeshi (literally, the ascetic's return). The abyss of the six realms is below them. Confession is the practice of the human realm. Aspiring to the world of light that is the kami and buddhas from the darkness of the six realms, practitioners crawl over a giant boulder which resembles Ama no Iwato, the rock door to the celestial cave.

Donryu

Arriving at a swamp intertwined with driftwood known as Donryu, practitioners enter the practice of the celestial realm which lies at the limit of the six realms. The echo of the golden bell blurs the lines between ignorance and sagehood, cutting away the causes and conditions for rebirth amidst the six realms. This ritual marks the boundary to the next dimension.

Shomon (Sravakabuddha)

The area known as Nenbutsu-Zawa is a mysterious landscape where celestial beings gather. At this place, practitioners offer incense to the kami and buddhas at the foot of the mountain, as well as to the ancestral lineage of practice at Koshikidake. Here, practitioners draw near to the voice of the kami and buddhas in their hearts at a shrine known as Chigaeshi.

Enkaku (Pratyekabuddha)

Straddling the abyss in a daze, practitioners arrive at the innermost secret part of the valley, the entrance to the grounds of the pratyekabuddha (enkaku). Here, they offer incense and recite the Verse of Original Enlightenment, avoiding the demons of conceit and self-satisfaction.

Bosatsu (Bodhisattva)

To aid the realisation of practitioners, a wondrous sutra of great merit is taught. Practitioners practice for the sake of revealing bodhi in order to bring benefit to others, that is, the resolution of a bodhisattva (bosatsu).

They make their way across a small pond called Chigaigaki and step into a profoundly sacred space. Here, there is an entrance to wakefulness. They offer incense again and chant the Verse of Original Enlightenment to avoid self-satisfaction. This secret place takes us to the final barrier called Omaedachi, where the kami and buddhas who protect the place are enshrined. This point symbolizes the simultaneous aspiration to bodhi (*jogu bodai*) and the vow to liberate beings *(geke shujo)*.

Buddha

Practitioners reach the Waterfall of the Three Honoured Ones, a secret place to form relationship with the kami and buddhas.

Performing *takigyo* (waterfall practice) they are struck by the waterfall, meditate and soak in the joy of the Dharma. Reciting the Sutra of Avalokitesvara, practitioners enter into the mind of compassionately enduring suffering for others. Holding this resolution closely, they return with the power of the bodhisattva.

Shugendo and the Martial Arts:

無垢清浄光
慧日破諸闇

The pure light of wisdom
illuminates the darkness

I receive many queries from people who want to know if there is a relationship between martial arts and Shugendo. I am neither a martial artist, nor a historian. I have no special exclusive knowledge, either. I briefly practiced Kendo in secondary school and I also have some experience with Taekwondo and Iaido (the art of drawing a sword). In this chapter, I will consider this topic within the limits of my personal understanding.

I studied and practiced the Shugen of Mt. Haguro for more than twenty years to revive the Shugendo of my family temple, based on Shinto-Buddhist combination *(shinbutsu shugo*). At Haguro, I once encountered a man who was both a priest and a martial artist. His real reason for visiting Haguro was to study the martial arts that he heard had been inherited by the Haguro lineage. He was very disappointed, however, to find that such a martial art did not exist. His great disappointment made him impatient and discouraged, but an old master priest suggested that he should test himself through committing himself to the Shugendo of Mt. Haguro. That was the beginning of his journey into Shugendo. He dedicated himself for several years and finally became a teacher-priest of Shugendo, too. At one time he told me that martial arts may not have been performed as a primary practice but rather as a Shugendo ceremony.

I cannot deny however that the martial arts have been deeply influenced by Shugendo throughout the ages because some schools of martial arts have inherited aspects of practices used in Shugendo, such as mudras and mantras. In these schools, these procedures are considered to be a very important part of practitioners mastering their martial art skills. One of the foundations of martial arts is the concept of *shin-gi-tai*, that is, 'heart/mind, technique and body'. This refers to the ability to control one's mind, body and technique as one, something which is closely related to religious philosophies handed down in Shugendo, Zen, esoteric Buddhism and Daoism.

The theory of *shin-gi-tai* is very similar to the theory of *sanmitsu*, the "three mysteries" of body, speech and mind. This refers to mudra, mantra and visualisation, which together constitute the foundation of ritual-practice in Shugendo.

The word *sanmitsu* can be found in the secret documents of the Shinkage-ryu school of martial arts. The *kuji-kiri* ("nine cuts") practice of Shugendo can also be found in the Katori-Shinden-ryu school, and in the Taisha-Ryu school, practitioners chant the mantra of the divinity Marishiten. The Itto-ryu school also uses the Buddhist "manji" (counter clockwise direction swastika) symbol as an important secret of swordsmanship.

Many founders of martial arts practiced deep in the mountains seeking a semblance of the divine. This is similar to the Way of Shugendo. But did the Shugendo sects inherit any kind of martial art or not? The priest I mentioned earlier suggested that practitioners who could not obey or follow the strict training of Shugendo may have joined wars as soldier-monks or spies. The period when Shugendo was establishing its doctrines and organisations was a period of great turbulence. From the end of the Heian period to the period of the Northern and Southern Courts (twelfth to fourteenth centuries), Japan was divided between the major powers of the Taira and the Minamoto and the Northern and Southern Dynasties. Battles were widespread and continuous all over Japan. Naturally, Yamabushi who knew the mountain trails in detail must have made excellent guides or spies. For this reason, some people regard Shugendo as the root of Ninja, although I have never found such historical material. But I believe that if there were these kinds of Yamabushi, they would have been very different from regular practitioners.

With this in mind, I would like to look at some of Shugendo's unique implements. There is a sword called *shiba-uchi* which Yamabushi used to carry. It looks more like a long hatchet with a single bevel blade. A long sword would have been to heavy and cumbersome to carry in the bush. Instead, it had to be small and tough like a survival knife used for wood-chopping. The *shiba-uchi* was also used in rituals and ceremonies. It was an all-purpose tool.

Yamabushi also carried with them a long wooden walking stick called a *kongo-jo* or vajra-staff. It measures roughly six feet in length. Some martial artists suggest that this stick was treated like a tool for self-defence because it can be used without killing someone. Stick fighting might have been part of the society of Shugendo.

There were other nomadic mountain societies in Japan too. One of them is referred to as *sanka*. The *sanka* were experts in wooden craftwork on which they relied to make a living. They also made a very special knife called an *umegai*. The *umegai* was long and triangular in shape with double edges on both sides. It could be useful for wood-chopping, woodwork and even for murder. *Umegai* could be an original form of the weapon of spies. In the deep mountains, very different tools had been used by special people. Across hundreds of years, it makes sense that they must have used these tools for something besides ritual ceremonies or daily chores.

As I mentioned earlier, the period of Shugendo's definition was one of great turbulence and war. To survive, Yamabushi might have taken sides with one of the two sides facing each other. Every religion in the world has a history of persecution. It is natural to think that Shugendo groupings which were operating or living in the mountain came to establish some special skills such as martial arts. During the Northern and Southern Courts period, the Emperor Go-Daigo left Kyoto and established his Southern Court in the impregnable mountains of Yoshino. The Shugendo groups operating there held their territory with the support of the Southern Court. Many Shugen temples here in Yamagata, far from Kyoto, had connections to the Southern Court through this mountain network. As evidence of this connection, there is a very old temple bell in Yamagata inscribed with the era name of the Southern Court. In the end, the courts were amalgamated, and the local Shugen sects which had supported the Southern Court gradually lost their power and influence.

Next, I would like to consider the connection between Shugendo and some well-known historical figures. The first is Minamoto no Yoshitsune (1159-1189), a samurai famously known as a tragic hero of the Heian period. Yoshitsune was a great strategist who was ultimately betrayed by his brother, Yoritomo. A legend says that Yoshitsune was trained in the art of swordsmanship by a tengu at Mt. Kurama. Tengu are legendary half-bird half-human creatures often depicted wearing the clothing of Yamabushi priests. It is said that the tengu are an expression of the Yamabushi who would practice to the limit of human ability.

The legend of Yoshitsune and the tengu may be an expression of the existence of armed groups of Yamabushi. Mt. Kurama was actually one of the largest Shugendo training centers at that time, and the school of swordsmanship known as Kurama-ryu still exists today. These legends suggest some relationship between Shugendo and the martial arts.

The other person I'd like to consider is Hayashizaki Jinsuke (1542-1621). Those who study Iaido swordsmanship recognise Hayashizaki as the restorer of one of the now-most widely practiced schools of Iaido in the world. He was born in Murayama City, Yamagata, which is also my hometown. Hayashizaki secluded himself in a cave on Mt. Koshikidake and devoted himself to improving his skill through praying to the great beings enshrined there. After 100 days, it is said that he attained a realisation which expressed itself as the Muso-Shinden school of swordsmanship. This school is the origin of many other styles of swordsmanship such as Muso-Jikiden-Eishin-ryu. Hayashizaki is considered to be a great grand-master of Iaido. His style of practice is similar to that in Shugendo in that both ways value sublime mental training and discipline. Not only Hayashizaki, but many other founders of martial arts undertook this kind of practice. With these situations in mind, it is evident that Shugendo and martial arts sometimes overlapped in a deep relationship, and I consider Mt. Koshikidake as a sacred place for martial arts because the divinities of Koshikidake initiated Hayashizaki into the mysteries of swordsmanship.

Previously, I never considered the relationship between Shugendo and martial arts and I could not understand why foreign martial artists were interested in Shugendo. It is an admirable situation, though often leads to confusion and mixed motivations for practice. There may be people promoting Shugendo in the West as a way to connect with the origin of some kind of lone warrior. I want to make it clear, however, that Shugendo is not this kind of thing. Those with motivations based on these kinds of ideas do not last and create many problems. The benefits of prayer and faith are not for ourselves. Those with an approach not based in bodhicitta and respect for the three jewels will ultimately be left disappointed.

我即阿毘羅吽欠

如次腰腹心額頂

This very body is abiraunken;
Seat, stomach, heart, forehead, and crown

Hashiramoto shinpo ("ritual method of offering to the pillars of the universe") is a secret practice unique to Shugendo based on the five elements which make up the body of the universe. The implements are very different from those used in esoteric Buddhism. The procedure itself decodes the origin of life and death and sublimates our very being.

This ritual-practice of *Hashiramoto shinpo* is said to have been taught through divine initiation by the Bodhisattva Nagarjuna in the mountains of Omine. It is the most secret ritual of Shugendo and can only be understood if one has practiced Shugendo for a considerable number of years under a direct teacher-disciple relationship. Here, I will leak some of the essence of this practice.

In this ritual, we offer ourselves to be united with the Buddha, Dainichi Nyorai (Mahavairocana). As this liturgy contains the great universe as the inner determination of Mahavairocana, it employs a completely different process of ritual prayer. That is, it is entirely different to the ritual prayer of esoteric Buddhism.

The secret essence of practice in Shugendo is hidden in this practice. Many of the texts associated with it were burned, destroyed in accordance with the kami-buddha separation orders of 1868. Today, there are quite a few sects attempting to revive this procedure based on old documents. It is a fact, however, that intentional mistakes, in some cases , have gone on to become part of the official liturgical procedure of a denomination. In some cases, it is taught merely as a matter of form in order to meet the requiremen-ts for obtaining priestly qualifications or ranking. For those who wish to understand its deeper truths, they may have to be taught again by someone who has mastered it.

This ritual procedure reveals the inner world of mountain training and the process of wakefulness. Through my more than twenty-five years of experience at Mt. Haguro, I realised that the inner dimension of mountain training is contained in the *hashiramoto shinpo* practice. However, many practitioners who know about it will never realise it. This procedure leads practitioners to the inner realisation of Shugendo; it is not only a ritual prayer but also a noble practice.

Hashiramoto shinpo is treated much like the goma ceremony of esoteric Buddhism, but it not an esoteric Buddhist goma. The goma of esoteric Buddhism is made up of various separate ritual actions. The procedure of *hashiramoto shinpo* on the other hand is the complete harmony between ritual prayer and the fire ceremony (*goma*). This version of the *hashiramoto* ritual is the one in the tradition of the Shugen of Dewa, that is, the old Shugendo found in modern day Yamagata. Today, apart from our denomination, an elderly priest living in Yamagata city is the only one to my knowledge performing this particular style of practice.

In contrast to esoteric Buddhism, which can be said to focus on the "cultivated awakening" of "Buddhahood in this very body" (*sokushin jobutsu* 即身成仏), Shugendo can be said to express the "original wakefulness" of "natural Buddhahood" (*jinen jobutsu* 自然成仏). Experiencing a spiritual death, everyone is able to realise awakening naturally.

Unlike the esoteric Buddhist altar, the *hashiramoto shinpo* can be performed using just thirty-seven wooden offerings; not many other offerings need to be prepared for this practice. Performing the regular goma requires around 200 wooden sticks and other kinds of offerings. Yamabushi generally perform ritual services at small temples or shrines and are financially not well-to-do. The *hashiramoto shinpo* can be performed in a way that is not so resource intensive, and it must have developed through being mindful of the support base of worshipers who, being common people, could not afford to request services at big temples.

In our denomination we first undertake the altar practices of the five honoured-ones which are taken as principal image (*honzon*): Fudo Myo-o (Acalanatha Vidyaraja), Juichimen Kannon (Ekadasamukha Avalokitesvara), Daikoku-ten (Mahakala), Bishamon-ten (Vaisravana) and Yakushi Nyorai (Bhaisajyaguru). As we become competent in these practices, we gradually learn more aspects of ritual prayer. While practicing these five procedures, practitioners can find their own tutelary deity and learn to understand the differences between each image. The goma fire for each procedure can be like a hot storm, a cold blizzard or a shower of light.

Hashiramoto shinpo is the process of "natural awakening" mentioned above and is undertaken through four ritual practices: "coming into existence" (*shokigyogi* 生起行儀), "gestating in the womb" (*tainai-gyogi* 胎内行儀), "outside the womb" (*taige-gyogi* 胎外行儀) and "death" (*shimetsu-gyogi* 死滅行儀). The practice moves from cause to effect and from effect to cause. There is no duality, just as there is no duality between a chicken and an egg. That which gives birth and that which is born are inseparable. Nothing happens if either one is missing. The same nonduality pertains, among others, to one's mother and father, the Womb and Vajra mandalas, the seed syllables A and Hum, Yin and Yang, and to all phenomena. This is symbolized through the use of ritual implements in the form of two wooden sticks called *nyumoku* (乳木). One contains the principle "from cause to effect" and the other "from effect to cause."

The first ritual practice, "coming into existence", begins when the two sticks are taken with both hands. The hands come together in a special mudra called *koshin gassho*, where the palms are placed together with the middle fingers held slightly apart, resembling the womb. The mantra of Mahavairocana and the five great elements is then recited. Coming into existence, we are part of the original enlightenment of Mahavairocana.

In the second practice, "gestating in the womb", we contemplate that the body begins to form. With the formation of sense perception and nerve tissue arise the defilements (kleshas, Jp. *bonno*) simultaneously with the aspiration to awakening (bodhicitta, Jp. *bodaishin*). In the third practice, "outside the womb", we chant the Verse of Original Enlightenment, which affirms this truth in our hearts. The fourth practice, "death", is a ritual of self-immolation. Entering into the mind of awakening, the practitioner burns away the body of the kleshas, offering them into the fire of the *saito goma*.

This series of practices gives a glimpse into the fundamental doctrine of Shugendo as expressed in the *hashiramoto shinpo*. It also shows how precious this human life is. We are born as ignorant beings. Despite this, even in the womb we possess all the virtues of the five elements of the universe. Outside of the womb, in the expanse of the universe, we must practice to recognise and awaken to this fundamental truth. Through practice, not intellectual-reasoning, we transform the body, made up as it is of the five elements, into the five-element stupa, that is, the stupa of the dharmadhatu, which is the body of the Buddha. The six elements of Mahavairocana are completed with the addition of consciousness to the aforementioned five. In the fire of self-cremation (*dabi*) one is able to recognise this consciousness, and the mandalic nature of the universe which expands endlessly. This may be impossible for us as ordinary, deluded beings, even if we do our best. This is the practice of Shugendo.

Shugendo is not a difficult belief-system to understand. It is a practice of the householder, where ordinary people practice for themselves to awaken to the dignity of life in nature and all things. Practitioners hone their minds and bodies by practicing the mountain asceticism of the "six perfections in the ten realms". Unlike other schools, Shugendo does not centre on a specific sutra or text. The secret of Shugendo is quite simple. Receiving life, growing in the womb, as human beings we are born and die. And amidst this we have the potential to awaken to the realisation of fundamental purity. You might be disappointed reading this. There is no occultism, glitz or glamour. You can find many books like that out there, but they are all fake; a fantasy.

The founder of Shingon Buddhism in Japan, Kukai (Kobo Daishi) is said to still be alive, having attained *sokushin-jobutsu* and practicing in meditation inside the inner precinct of Mount Koya, Shingon's head temple. Meals and clothing are still offered to him every day. At Mount Yudono's Dainichibo temple, Shinnyokai Shonin (真如海上人) is also said to have attained *sokushin jobutsu*, but he is dead. He is representative of the Yudono lineage and is enshrined as a mummified buddha-figure who vows to alleviate the suffering of beings before and after death. In the eighteenth century, Shinnyokai practised severe asceticism and towards the end of his life finally settled himself into the ground while still alive, eating only wild vegetables and raw nuts. This practice was undertaken with a readiness to die. Around 150 years later there was another practitioner who undertook a similar practice at Mt. Koshikidake named Kokai Shonin (1596-1658). He practiced in the Senninzawa area of Mt. Yudono, noted as a site for extreme ascetic practices, including abstention from cereals and eating only pine needles and bark (*mokujikigyo*).

Kokai Shonin was known for his constant work for the good of the community, among which was the construction of a stone pass in Tsuruoka called Dainichi Toge. It can still be seen and a stone there is inscribed with his named to honour his memory. In 1657, the Kannonji Temple on Mt Koshikidake was struck by lightning and burned down. Kokai set to work rebuilding it and used Mt. Koshikidake and the area of Murayama as his base to spread his teachings among the people. The inhabitants of this region held him in great honour.

Kokai Shonin generated a great reputation for Dewa Sanzan. He was a great friend of the superintendent priest of Haguro, Tenyuu (1595–1675), who placed the Shugendo shrine-temple complex at Mt. Haguro under supervision of the Tendai school in order to preserve its independence from the official Tozan and Honzan groupings. Today, he is considered the second 'opener' of the mountain. Koshikidake Kannonji temple holds a scroll painted by Tenyuu, signed by him as the superintendent priest of Mt. Haguro.

In 1658, after a life of religious cultivation, Kokai began a period of fasting, ending in a cavern on Mt. Koshikidake. He entered meditative absorption and died in 1658. The people of the time requested that Kokai leave his *yuigesa* (surplice) to preserve his memory. Three hundred and fifty years later, the original yuigesa has been restored and serves as one of the current designs used at Kannonji today. The yuigesa has six Dharma wheels in the style of Tozan-ha Shugen. The Three Mountains of Dewa are symbolised respectively as the three-legged crow which guided Nojo Taishi to Mt. Haguro (birth), a rabbit (Mt. Gassan - death) and a blossom (Mt. Yudono - rebirth).

Shugendo is a practice open to all. For professional priests who are active in Shugendo, it can be like an open-weight division boxer fighting in the middle-weight division ring and bragging, "I'm the best!" This kind of ridicule is not uncommon. In the past, esoteric Buddhist priests would make fun of Shugendo. In fact, once an old esoteric Buddhist priest hissed at me saying, "Lowly Yamabushi!" He perceived Shugendo as a bastardisation of Buddhahood and may have thought that I was a negligent practitioner.

Reading this, you may be thinking, "Is Shugendo then an inferior practice?" The answer is no, that is not true. The practice path of Shugendo cannot be undertaken unless one is keenly aware of one's shortcomings and is prepared to do one's best in resolving an eternal practice for the rest of one's life. To say one is busy with work or to practice only when one has time is not a good motivation. These people are not suitable for the five elements practice of Shugendo.

In finishing, I would like to reveal to you the ultimate secret of my Shugendo practice. You must not reveal it, as it is a maxim which expresses the essence of the *hashiramoto* practice. Please listen carefully and remember it when you feel lazy:

Only death will cure a fool.

A REFLECTION ON MOUNTAIN TRAINING

MEIDO MOORE

In 2019, I was privileged to enter Mt. Koshikidake for the first time, training under the guidance of Koshikidake Soke and his students. Since that time, with Soke's further guidance, we have also been able to establish something remarkable: *gyoba*, training fields, for Shugendo Mountain Training in North America and Europe. I would therefore like to share my thoughts about this experience of Mountain Training, hoping that it will be interesting and encouraging to others.

We know of course that Mt. Koshikidake, near Higashine City in Yamagata Prefecture, has a unique history. The mountain was venerated at least from the Nara period for its location in the direction of the *kimon*, or "demon gate," of that early capital, serving thus to protect it from negative spiritual forces. At 1016 meters it is not high compared to some of Japan's mountains. But the terrain is quite rugged: undulating, deeply forested ridges give the appearance of a dragon's back, rising to a central peak which is almost pyramidal in shape.

I soon learned that ascending that peak requires care. This ascent in fact takes place on the first day of the three-day training. Beginning with an opening ceremony at the shrine of the Yama no Kami, the deity of the mountain, our group of 26 *shugenja* walked in a procession that was at first relaxed and joyful. But in fact, this is a kind of funeral procession. Arriving soon after at a bridge spanning one of the mountain streams, we began to walk in silence with a mood of calm seriousness, for in crossing that bridge we departed from our everyday lives and entered the mandala of the mountain.

Though we may not share ritual details of the mountain training, I can speak a bit about its general pattern. What the practice allows is a bodily experience of the Ten Realms (*jukkai*). In Buddhist thought these are the ten general ways in which sentient beings are reborn, lifetime after lifetime, from the lowest realms of hellish suffering up to the highest summit of awakening. Of course, one may also cycle through these modes of existence within a single day or even a few moments of time, as the Mountain Training makes quite clear. But though one may conceptually understand this teaching of *jukkai*, it is quite another thing to re-enact and experience each realm in turn with one's own body and senses - and most importantly, to do so within the community of fellow shugenja.

There is a time during the training, for example, when the group enters a situation of oppressive suffering. Within a small, enclosed space, surrounded by one's dharma brothers and sisters and experiencing one's own discomfort joined with that of the others, one can indeed truly feel the reality of a hellish realm. At another time, since almost no food and little sleep is permitted for a few days, the realm of the hungry spirits – that is, a mode of being marked by craving and despair – becomes something quite real to the practitioner. When a moment then comes that a small bit of food is given, one suddenly finds oneself in a realm of great bliss and enjoyment. All of the training is like this, and so naturally each activity and ritual becomes a mirror within which one's own fixations, obstructions, weaknesses, and strengths can be clearly seen. In other words, we do not just re-enact the Ten Realms; we are each made to see our habitual patterns that manifest those realms within our own minds and bodies. We can, perhaps for the first time, clearly see the patterns of our own karmic traces (*jikke*) within which we have been unconsciously entwined our whole lives. The training serves as a mirror in this way.

But there is something else revealed, and this I think is the real treasure that one brings down from the mountain. One comes to see that this training is not done by, or for, oneself at all. That is, we think in the beginning that we enter the mountain to do *shugyo*—profound training of body and mind—in order to improve ourselves, or to gain something of value for our own lives. We think that we are ascending the mountain using the power of our own feet. But the truth is quite different. During the mountain training one's primary concern, in fact, completely ceases to be what one is experiencing for oneself. Instead, it becomes joined with all the others who are there with us, as each trainee attends with great care to one another, helping to pull and push each other past obstacles and through each difficult trial. In this way, we begin to feel not only that the other practitioners lift us up, but that the mountain itself is something supporting our feet. We can realize that the mountain is not an obstacle to be climbed, a thing that we conquer with our steps as a kind of challenge. We know instead that the mountain lifts us to its own summit and embraces us all completely.

Perhaps most importantly, this transcendence of self-fixation extends beyond the mountain. There is a moment when, looking down from the summit to the world far below—that is, to the mundane world one has seemingly left behind—the group chants the sutra of Kannon (the bodhisattva of compassion) for all beings. One can understand then that this rarefied mountain world only exists and has meaning in relationship with the one below. Shugendo is thus not, as some probably imagine, a solitary practice of mountain hermits, who ascend to uninhabited, lonely places to work out their individual spiritual realization. I think now that even in the most remote, secret practice places on the mountain, the shugenja of ancient times must have maintained community with one another, and kept constantly in their minds the world below. Though we ascend to the peak, in fact it is the descent that follows—a returning to the world—that reveals what mountain training truly is.

In the end, one comes to see that the training was not a case of "entering" the mountain and then "returning" from it with something. It was to realize the mandala of the mountain within one's life, and to manifest the shining clarity of the summit in all the realms, and for all the people, one encounters each day. It is a practice to unify all mandala worlds within this very body.

As I am also a Zen practitioner, I would here also like to say that especially in this respect the path of Shugen and the path of Zen are not in conflict at all. In Zen we say that the true Way is one of "simultaneously reaching up and reaching down"; that is, as one ascends to ever more deeply integrated realization, one simultaneously reaches down to lift up others. The end of the Zen path is not some exalted state of solitary realization, but to become completely natural, "bare-chested and barefoot, returning to the marketplace," to dispense the gift of fearlessness (*se mu-i*) to the people. As I think of the history of the Koshikidake family, which for many generations served as village shugenja priests administering to the needs of the community, I believe this is precisely the same.

In regard to "simultaneous reaching up and down," in fact there was one occasion on the mountain that brought this saying to mind in a rather literal manner. There was a moment while walking that I happened to let my concentration wander, at which point I suddenly stumbled, falling off the path and down a steep slope, grasping at trees and bushes to stop my slide. But in an instant, several pairs of hands reached down from above to help me. Later, it happened I had the chance to aid someone else like this. And so all together in this way, each at his own pace but with no one left behind, every single participant succeeded in reaching the peak.

This reminds me also of another occasion, the time I mentioned earlier during which all the shugenja experience a kind of hellish suffering together. Though initially one is absorbed in one's own discomfort, remarkably after a time there is a shift: one finds oneself recognizing the suffering of those nearby, and suddenly a great compassion for them arises, as one's own suffering becomes of secondary importance. Truly, in the midst even of a hell realm, the precious arising of *bodaishin* – the aspiration for liberation for all beings – blossoms, like a lotus in the fire. This is indeed the root of all Buddhist paths, and during the Mountain Training it is something experienced profoundly with one's body.

Ascending the mountain is only the first day of the training. Throughout the two days that follow there are many hours of ritual and other practice, culminating finally in the *saito goma* ceremony. Many local people came to see and participate in this, and so the shugenja are able to formally bring the blessings of their practice to everyone using the ritual. It is a fitting way for the training to end: with the summit of the mountain and the town below seamlessly joined. To experience this bodhisattva activity in company with practitioners coming from places as varied as Japan, Australia, Canada, Malaysia, and USA, was incredibly beautiful.

There are many more things that could be said. But I hope this brief account from a beginner will encourage anyone to attend Mountain Training. People of widely varied ages and conditions could complete it. It is difficult, but it is not too difficult. There is no doubt that you can discover your own strength and achieve this goal.

But more importantly, as I described, I believe you could realize that your goal and your life is not yours alone, and that together with the community of practitioners—and all the people, animals, plants, and all beings everywhere—we have always been together on the mountain. Mountain Training is a Shugendo practice to fundamentally change one's orientation: to lay down one's body and self-fixation completely on the mountainside, and to be reborn within nature to a new life that can be of use to others. As Koshikidake Soke said at one point, "We should not think about our practice, 'What do I want to do?' We should think, 'What do the buddhas and deities want me to do?'"

Though it sounds simple, this is a very profound statement revealing not only the way to practice, but a way to live. If you would like to experience this for yourself, please come and join us on the mountain.

A BRIEF HISTORY OF KOSHIKIDAKE KANNONJI

RICCO (JISHO) SCHROER

Mount Koshikidake is a dormant volcano located in modern day Yamagata Prefecture, in what is now Murayama City at the Western tip of the Ou Mountain range. It is a modest mountain, rising for approximately 5km, reaching a total altitude of 1,016 meters. Today, Mt. Koshikidake is largely known as a popular hiking spot through its inclusion among the 100 famous mountains of Tohoku. This mountain, however, also carries a hidden history, both as a "*kimon*" mountain and as a site significant to Shugendo.

In the past, Mt. Koshikidake was a popular site of worship due to its associations with various deities as well as Avalokitesvara-faith. With the separation of Shinto and

Buddhism in the Meiji era, however, the religious colour of the mountain gradually faded. Mount Koshikidake's trails are said to have been significant to the indigenous Ezo people dating back to the Jomon period and traces of ancient well sites have been found across the mountain. The characters *koshiki* carry the meaning of a rice cooker, which the peak (*dake*) is said to resemble. The seal of Koshikidake consists of a circle surrounded by eight more circles, resembling a wheel and its hub, and symbolises the nine luminaries (Skt. *navagraha*; Jp. *kuyo*).

Traditionally revered as the abode of the *mikumari* deity (divinity of water) and as a site of *amagoi* (rain making), songs of praise (*sanka*) passed down over the centuries speak to the prominent role rain ceremonies played in the mountain's culture. Since the introduction of Buddhism, worship related to Avalokitesvara in various manifestations has always been popular in the region, in part due to Avalokitesvara's relationship with rain-making. Dragons and *nagas* are also related to rainmaking and traditionally Mt Koshikidake's manifestation was worshipped as *Koshikidake Gongen-Suiten-Ryu-o* ('Water-Deva Dragon-King'), with the *ground form* (*honji*) of Avalokitesvara.

Buddhism's emergence and the 'opening' of Buddhist practice at Mt. Koshikidake is traditionally attributed to Dosho Shonin (629-700), a semi-legendary monk considered to be among the founding figures of Buddhism in Japan. In 653, he was supported by the emperor to travel to China where he studied Yogacara and Chan under the Buddhist monk Xuanzang (602-664), whose travels to India have been immortalized in the book *Journey to the West.* There is an episode in a book of *setsuwa* (stories of miraculous happenings) compiled in the ninth century that describes how Dosho, while in China, visited the Kingdom of Silla (Korea) where he lectured on the Lotus Sutra. Here he met a man 'among the tigers' who offered up a question in the Japanese language. The man declared himself to be *En no Ubasoku* (En no Gyoja), the legendary patriarch of Shugendo.

Early in his lifc, Dosho is said to have roamed the Japanese archipelago, devoting himself to works that contributed to the welfare of the public. It was during this time, at around age twenty, that he sought out a mountain at Imperial request to act as a *kimon* for the capital. The *kimon* is associated with the north-east direction and Mt. Koshikidake sits in this direction from the capital at the time (Asuka, Nara). According to *Onmyodo* (yin-yang style divination & geomancy), north-east is considered a particularly taboo direction through which malevolent forces are able to enter and leave. Shrines and temples in this cardinal direction were established to act as *kimon 'demon-gates'* in order to seal malevolent influences and Koshikidake Kannonji acted in this role for centuries. Dosho's actions are said to have led to the enshrining of Avalokitesvara at Mt. Koshikidake and the opening of the Hakko-in temple, the predecessor of the later Kannonji temple.

Shugendo appeared in the Dewa basin with the transference of the three deities of Kumano to the mountains of Dewa and, according to legend, with Nojo Taishi's 'opening' of the three mountains of Dewa during his ascetic seclusions. Historically, the triad of *Dewa-Sanzan* has included Mt. Gassan, Mt. Chokai, Mt. Haguro, Mt. Hayama and Mt. Yudono. While the three deities of Kumano are considered emanations of Bhaisajyaguru (*yakushi*), Amitabha (*amida*), and Ekadasamukha Avalokitesvara (*juichimen kannon*), their manifestation in the Dewa region appeared as Bhaisajyaguru (*yakushi*), Amitabha (*amida*), and Arya-Avalokitesvara (*sho-kannon*).

In a mirroring of this tradition, these three figures were also enshrined at Mount Koshikidake. Kannonji temple shifted to the foot of the mountain in the first year of the Onin era (1467) and became a village-temple in the third year of the Kan'en era (1755). During this period, the temple was added as an 'extra stop' (#36) on the Thirty-Three Avalokitesvara Pilgrimage of Mogami and flourished as a site of pilgrimage.

Shugendo at Koshikidake Kannonji developed both through its connections with Dewa Sanzan as well as its Edo period affiliation with the Tozan stream of Shugendo based out of Daigoji Sanboin. Documents held by Kannonji show that during this period the boundaries between sect identities weren't so clear and that shugenja enroute to sites of practice stopped at many different kinds of temples and had mentors and teachers that varied across sectarian divisions. Buddhist family records (*kakocho*) dating from the early Edo period indicate that the temple priests of Kannonji were married.

The following origin story (*engi*) is recorded in the History of Tateoka City (*tateokamachi rekishi*) held in the collection of Kaitanji Temple in Murayama City:

> "Thirteen hundred years ago in the in the Taika era (648), Dosho Shonin enshrined a spiritual image at Mount Koshikidake. With the advent of Kobo Daishi, esoteric Buddhism was brought to the mountain. The Shugen-Dharma of En no Gyoja was transmitted to Mt Koshikidake via Rigen Daishi [Shobo] of Daigo-ji temple."

With the advent of the Meiji period, the government at the time sought to match the ideological threat of Western modernity. Part of these reforms involved the clarification and separation of Shinto and Buddhism into distinct bodies. Before the Meiji Restoration, shrines were disorganised institutions usually attached to Buddhist temples. Under the Meiji period *separation orders* (*shinbutsu-bunri*) however, they were turned into independent, systematised institutions. The separation orders triggered the *haibutsu kishaku* (Expulsion of Buddhism and Sakyamuni Movement), a violent anti-Buddhist movement which caused the forcible closure and burning of thousands of temples, the confiscation of their land, the forced return of many monks and yamabushi to lay life or their transformation into Shinto priests, and, the destruction of numerous books, statues, combinatory practices and artefacts. Temples were also prohibited from practicing rites that were now declared to be Shinto, with many ritual texts being destroyed or dislocated from their original contexts.

Shugendo was outlawed and banned outright in 1872, being a typical case of the 'mixture' of Buddhism and Shinto. The priests of Shugendo shrine-temple complexes were forced to choose to laicize, become Shinto shrine attendants or Buddhist priests and their practices were banned. It is no stretch to say that this process was world-shattering to the beliefs and worldviews of the time, with the newly approved version of Shinto being a heavily distorted version of what previously existed, reconfigured to support a new mythology presented as representing an unbroken imperial tradition. This period of Shugendo's history is characterised by its suppression and subsequent varying degrees of resistance, compromise, collaboration and absorption by other sects. In this context, Kannonji temple was converted into a shrine and its attendant shugenja were converted into Shinto-Shrine priests. As a shrine, Kannonji was restructured to conform to the new Shinto orthodoxy and was officially dedicated to the deity Sukunahikona no Mikoto.

The last superintendent (*betto*) of Kannonji was Kanryu, who laicised in 1871 as Koshikidake Motoi and became a shrine priest. His son, Ishimi, continued as the shrine priest of Koshikidake Jinja, but hardships and financial problems forced him to sell some of the family's inherited items to support himself. Ishimi would go on to die of tuberculosis before reaching old age. His son, Kojiro, worked in the city office but continued this legacy, performing combinatory rites and memorialization services, as well as ground breaking and rain making rituals. In times of drought, he would climb Mt. Koshikidake to offer prayers and his son Ikuo would join him. Ikuo is the father of Shodo, the current head-priest spearheading the temple's revival; a task which was wished upon him by his grandmother, Shiu.

Despite the dismantling of Koshikidake Kannonji, Buddhist statues, images and documents were kept in secret and combinatory style practice was carried out under the outer guise of a Shinto Priest. These documents were passed carefully down the generations to the present. The main *Zenko-ji* style image of Arya-Avalokitesvara is still preserved and is now held at the current Kannonji temple in nearby Murayama city. The documents which have been preserved represent a rich storehouse of information about the activities, both religious and secular, of an Edo period Shugen priest. Shugendo historian and practitioner, Gaynor Sekimori, writes:

> Kannonji's rich archive contains letters related to shipping along the Mogami river, documents concerning village administration and education, Yoshida Shinto and Onmyodo licenses, sutras and divination manuals, plus more than 600 ritual manuals detailing the veneration of various deities (mostly according to the Ono-ryu of Shingon) and a large number of Ryobu Shinto manuals, setting out rites such as the ground-breaking ceremony.

> It has a very rich archival collection, consisting both of ritual manuals, mainly from the Daigoji and Negoroji (Shingi Shingon) lineages, and a large amount of eighteenth and nineteenth century documents which attest to the diverse role occupied by village-based shugenja (*sato shugen/mappa shugen*). ("Defining Shugendo Past and Present," *Cahiers d'Extreme-Asie* 2009, p. 49).

For Shodo, restoring Shugendo is above all about restoring the old mountain routes (and by extension, practices associated with *shinbutsu-shugo*). But equally important for the future of the revived Shugendo is that participants, by performing such practices as shugenja, gain a sense of cohesion. This re-establishment of identity is a core theme within modern Shugendo. The restoration of ritual practice, meditation, mountain-entry, and the ascetic training of members through it, has been at the core of Shugendo's revival in general.

Concerning the revival of Shugendo in Japan, and at Mt. Koshikidake in particular, Gaynor Sekimori writes:

> With the ongoing discovery of archival material, dating in the main from after the seventeenth century, much more is becoming known about Shugendo networks, lifestyles and organization in the early modern period, and it can no longer be sustained that there is nothing of interest to study in Shugendo after the "itinerant yamabushi" idealized by Wakamori

was no longer the paradigm of a shugenja. The work of Kanda Yoriko and her team in the villages around Mt Chokai (on the Yamagata/Akita border) [has uncovered] a great wealth of material for understanding the life of the yamabushi in the area and their activities. Family and temple records such as the Arayama, Nanshóji and Daisen'in archives are being used to trace such things as the activities of *sendatsu* (pilgrim guides) and the involvement of yamabushi in village ritual.

New collections are being discovered regularly and await scholarly attention. One example is the Koshikidake archive (Higashine, Yamagata), some 600 documents belonging to the descendants of the priests of the Tozan-ha temple, Kannonji, which disappeared in the early Meiji period to become a Shinto shrine. Besides ritual texts, which are being used to reconstruct the lost traditions of the temple, there is a wealth of documentation concerning the life of a Shugendo priest in the early modern period – exchanges with the civil authorities, land registers, taxation documents, communications with the head temple, trading papers, religious licenses, and so on. ("Shugendo: Japanese Mountain Religion – State of the Field and Bibliographic Review", *Religion Compass*. January 2009, p. 39)

A study carried out in 2010 by Gaynor Sekimori sheds light on the composition and motivation of participants in the early period of the revival.

> "Koshikidake has around twenty disciples (*deshi*). They vary in occupation, and include an industrial designer, civil servant, company manager, estate agent, soba cook, taxi driver, transport manager, civil engineer, high school teacher, and masseur. The proportion of men to women is about 3:2. They come from all over Japan, including Tokyo, Kobe, Nara, Nagoya, Shizuoka, Kyushu and Yamagata, and all have different reasons for joining, mostly unrelated to any idea of Shugendo ... Most are attracted to the idea of being able, as lay people, to learn and perform rituals and come into direct contact with the deities (*kaji kito*). For example, a Tochigi construction manager wanted to be able to venerate his own ancestors himself, a Sapporo nurse wanted to learn ancestral veneration rites so she could memorialize those of her patients who had died, and a female office worker from Nagoya [with marriage problems] after receiving instruction in the Daikoku ritual, decided to become a deshi in order to attain the spiritual authority to pray for women in particular. On the other hand, a karate teacher from Yamagata joined in order to gain mental and physical strength through ascetic practice.
>
> Koshikidake's website has also been an important method of information and recruitment. It was through it that a former *yakuza* from Kyushu, who is now a

company manager, discovered that he would be able to do the traditional post-ordination training that had been denied to him elsewhere. He had been drawn to Buddhism while in prison and on his release determined to go straight. Deciding that in order to do this he needed the intervention of the kami and buddhas, he took ordination at a local temple affiliated with Mount Koya, but was refused permission to do post-ordination training at the head temple because of his tattoos and other reminders of his past. Both the above-mentioned Nagoya office worker and the Sapporo nurse found out about these group through the website. Others have done so by meeting Koshikidake at lecture meetings or through personal recommendations. An example of the former is a company manager who was troubled by the personal relations involved in his job, and the latter the mother and son of the Tochigi construction manager mentioned above.

In addition to disciples there are around 70 families (130 people) who are devotees (parish supporters). These are mainly local people, from Yamagata and neighbouring Miyagi, who have come to know of Koshikidake through word of mouth." ("Defining Shugendo," p. 62)

Throughout Mt. Koshikidake's history it has been strongly associated with harvest-divinity (作 神 ; *sakujin*) and Avalokitesvara-faith. At the height of Mt. Koshikidake's popularity, the Niiyama and Nakazawa districts of

Murayama City acted as the main pilgrimage trailheads. Prior to the Meiji period, Murayama was a temple town with many temple lodgings, a history which is still evident today through the presence of stone torii gates and stone monuments dedicated to Haguro.

Temples associated with Shugen and esoteric Buddhism faced the frequent threat of complete destruction throughout the power-struggles of the Kamakura period, the period of the Northern and Southern Courts, as well as during the Muromachi period. Not only were buildings demolished, but those that were aligned with the losing side often saw stone-monuments, cornerstones and the foundations of temples completely erased, destroying any memory of their existence. In this context, Koshikidake Kannonji was cleverly able to extend its life-expectancy by aligning itself with the Southern Court all the way up to the Meiji period anti-Buddhist persecutions and separation orders. At Haguro, the impact of this period can still be seen through the remnants of many decapitated stone buddhas tossed into the scrub as well as stone tablets with Siddham (Bonji) script scraped off.

Deep in Mt. Koshikidake there is a river which old maps held by the temple identify using the name *Shimoanja*. The term *anja* here means *ascetic* (行者; *gyōja*). Old documents held by Kannonji also show that there was a waterfall known as *Takizawa-Okami* (滝 沢 大 神) associated with Aryacalanatha Vidyaraja which functioned as a main training-ground for practitioners. Today, however, this area barely runs with water due to it being redirected towards the district's water supply. Off the main trail near the ruins of an old gold-mine is a site called *Passing Through the Womb* (胎内くぐり; *tainaikūguri*) which mirrors the Haguro site of *higashi-fudaraku*. Near here, too, is a cliff-hanging rock-site associated with the practice of confession, known as *Ksitigarbha Rock* (地蔵岩; *jizōiwa*). These are just a few examples of many sacred sites in the mountain, which, with great effort, are being revitalised. During the Meiji period separation orders, these practice sites were all left out of documents which had to be submitted to the commissioner responsible for overseeing the 'separation' of temples and shrines.

> The way the ritual practices, particularly those associated with mountain-entry, have been revived aptly demonstrates the contrast between premodern and modern *shugenja*. While both are described as "neither fully clerical nor fully lay" (*hanso hanzoku*) the nature of their identity is bound up in the social mores of the different times. Edo period *shugenja* were, on the whole, ordained priests who happened to have families. They were professionally bound to their position as *shugenja*, and most supervised village temples or small shrines and halls. They advanced in rank according to the number of mountain-entry practices they did. This is the pattern associated with the priests of Kannonji at Koshikidake. The Nikko situation was somewhat different, in that the *shugenja* affiliated with Rinnoji

could perhaps best be described as salaried workers, with specific duties and responsibilities to the temple. Thus the long and time-consuming practice circuits, for example, were part of their workload. Modern Shugendo cannot support "professional" shugenja, and full-time ordained priests in Shugendo temples such as Kinpusenji are greatly in the minority. It is important, therefore, that Shugendo takes into account the fact that the majority of its practitioners work for a living. ("Defining Shugendo," p. 64)

Concerning the revival of Shugendo at Mt. Koshikidake in particular, there has been one major shift in the modern understanding of Shugendo: the relationship between belief and nature.

"The annual mountain-entry practice was devised to teach [students] a Shugendo world-view and to bring them to a realization that belief and nature merge. Koshikidake readily admits there is a social element here, teaching the deeper meaning of environmental protection ... Whereas in the past the mountain was the realm of the dead, a place where spiritual power was gained through contact with the deities, today mountain beliefs are equated very much with nature and the environment. That is, the mountain is also framed as a place where people can go to experience "nature". It is not an accident that Shugendo claims contemporary relevance (as does Shinto) as an environmentally responsible movement. ("Defining Shugendo", pp. 70-71)

The Shugendo of Koshikidake-Kannonji undertakes to teach practitioners the Shugendo world view and exposing them to ritual prayer (*kaji kito*) in action by taking them into the mountain, and to this end has been holding an annual mountain (and valley) ritual at Mt Koshikidake since 2006. The revival of Shugendo there emphasises "the restoration of pre-Meiji combinatory rituals, the reinvigoration of *shinbutsu shugo* as the core of Japanese religious life," honouring his shugenja ancestors, and creating the kind of information networks that operated among *shugenja*, and "the recovery, before they are lost forever, of Shugendo practices such as ways of blowing the *horagai* and patterns of cutting *gohei*", both of whose traditions have been orally transmitted and now there are few left to continue them. At the centre of his efforts is the conviction that there is too great a gap between belief and everyday life. "Because Shugendo allows people to gain a high degree of spiritual attainment within the lay life, and to pass on their attainments for the benefit of the community through performing rituals, it seems very well suited to contemporary needs." ("Defining Shugendo," p. 71)

Training at Kannonji takes form through a hierarchy of practices and ritual-manners. These include a variety of altar practices centred on different main deities, as well as *jingi* (kami) manners, the incense goma, *juhachido*, *ajikan* and *hashiramoto shinpo*. Learning these manners is undertaken within the student-teacher relationship based on ordination and various forms of abhiseka (*kanjo*). Titles and rankings in the denomination are obtained based both on the deepening of ritual practice and through participation in annual mountain and valley training.

Shodo has also garnered international interest through his bilingual online presence. Over the years, many foreigners have come to experience mountain-training, with some going on to become personal students of Koshikidake. In this

way, Kannonji has over time produced a number of branch priests active outside of Japan. These include Jisho Schroer (Australia), Meido Moore (USA), Kanjin Cederman (USA) and Eikai Ip (Canada). International collaboration has seen priests from Kannonji as well as Mitsunaga Dai Ajari take part in events at Seisoin-Tenmyoji temple in Canada and at Korinji temple in the USA, giving participants the chance to experience teachings as well as aspects of mountain training, such as the *Saito Goma* ceremony.

Each of these practitioners have vastly different reasons for entering Kannonji temple. For Kanjin Cederman, a Nichiren-shu priest, the desire to experience on a deeper level the aspects of Shugen he had encountered in his traditional Nichiren training was a great motivating factor, a project which has seen the development of the Seattle Mountain Training Center.

> "In my tradition, there was once an associated Shugendo practice called Hokke Shugen (Lotus Shugen). Within modern Nichiren Shu Buddhism there are many aspects and remnants of this tradition still alive today, including the importance of sacred mountains and the use of the *bokken* and *juzu* during *kito* prayers and purification ceremonies."

At Koshikidake Kannonji, there is no discrimination based on age, gender, race, creed, or national origin. However, candidates are forewarned not to pursue religion as a career or for financial gain. Koshikidake's role model for modern shugenja remains En no Gyoja, and his ideal is the traditional householder who is at once part of the secular world as well as the religious realm at the same time (*hanzo hanzoku*). Koshikidake puts this as follows:

> "While at Shozen'in [Haguro], I was working as a news reporter. I had to leave the mountain to cover parliamentary elections. After covering that news, I would return straight back to Haguro. This crossing over of two worlds is the Shugen Way. Faith supports our everyday life. Supposing we make our faith an occupation, what then does this faith support? This is a petty life. Shugendo above all is a faith for common people.
>
> Members of our temple are farmers, housewives, office workers, teachers and so on. We are not special people, we are ordinary persons studying and

helping each other. There remains some Shugen temples in Japan like this. They continue to make efforts to brush up their faith every day. Living in the world of *samsara* involves becoming polluted, and one cannot spiritually assist or aid others without knowing the trials and tribulations of everyday life through one`s own experience. By knowing the joys and miseries of the human condition directly, the Shugen practitioner recognizes the necessity of spiritual assistance and training, especially purification and repentance."

五蘊盛苦

To know the limits
of great suffering
until it is relieved.

I was born in Hokkaido on the seventh of October in 1958. In Buddhism, it is said that the dead wander in an intermediate state for 49 days. Around that day, 49 days before my birthday, there was a massacre in Tibet, and the Dalai Lama fled to India the following year. It is curious that there are many Yamabushi around me who were also born in 1958. To me, this suggests the possibility that they may have come back to this world in order to raise the Buddha's Dharma.

I am a descendant of Kanryu (Koishikidake Motoi), the last head-priest of Kannonji who laicised in 1871. My father, Koshikidake Ikuo, was a high school science teacher in a small fishing village in Hokkaido, where I lived until the third grade. There was no religious atmosphere around me at that time. I was an odd boy who dreamed that a huge whale would come to pick me up from far across the sea. I was foolish and innocent, once accidentally playing and digging in a graveyard.

One day a strange event occurred when my friends and I escaped from kindergarten. We wandered across a waste field, through a dark wood and eventually arrived at a small shrine. We got excited because our plan was to break open the door and find what treasure could be found inside. We approached the shrine slowly, checking to make sure nobody else was around. Suddenly the door of the shrine made a loud noise and the big bell hanging in front of the shrine began to ring. Our secret plan had been ruined! Somebody was there to scold us! We gave up and gazed through the door. "Nobody's there! It's a ghost!" My friends took off, but I was paralysed with terror and my knees gave way. I was left alone in the shrine precinct and saw in front of me a strange vision. Before my eyes was a boundless blue grass field. Thunder broke out in the violet sky and the bright red shrine towered over me. With the appearance of a shrine maiden (*miko*), I had no choice but to stand. All of a sudden, I realized that I was standing in the grounds of the kindergarten with my friends who had accompanied me to the shrine. They were playing as if nothing had happened.

When I was in the fourth grade, I moved away from my parents to live with my grandmother in Yamagata. My grandmother maintained my family's religious customs with a deep sense of faith. She is ultimately the reason why I continued the Shugendo of my family. In Yamagata, people spoke with a strong dialect, so much so that I could not understand what they were saying because I was used to speaking the standard Japanese spoken in Hokkaido. Yamagata was like entering a foreign country. It is from my grandmother that I learned the foundations of my family's religious tradition. She taught me to recite sutras and *norito* from both Shinto and Buddhism and I would recite them daily as a matter of course. Despite my grandmother's scolding, I would often invite over a Christian missionary and listen to him while she was away. I spent a lot of time in the house and it did not take long to start feeling something that I was unable to see. There is a Japanese legend regarding a spirit-child called *zashiki warashi* which is believed to protect the house and who has been passed down across generations. I would often hear the piano playing, the sound of footsteps running upstairs and the voice of a child saying,

"*Tadaima*!" (I am home) despite being alone in the house. I would tell the Christian missionary about these stories and they would scare him. In exchange he would relate stories from the Bible to me.

As I became accustomed to living in Yamagata, I began to go on adventures through the back streets of the district and abandoned reciting sutras. I would climb up Mt. Koshikidake which rose high above the town. Getting out of the modest town and walking along the mulberry fields, I made my way through the cryptomeria forest where the smells of the grasses and woods aroused my senses. The air of the forest made me feel like I was travelling through another world. The sounds of the mountain stream and birds among the larches were music to my ears. I was easily able to reach the top of the mountain and would quench my thirst from the spring as I made my way through the chestnut forest near the site of the old Kannonji temple. One day, I almost got lost due to a sudden fog enveloping me. I found myself standing in an open area where an old hall stood among the woods. There was a stone lantern beside the hall. When I arrived home later, I told my grandmother about what I had seen in the mountain. She suggested that I should offer a candle and place it in the lantern. I tried to find that place again, however it was nowhere to be found. After several attempts, I finally found the lantern and offered candles there, but this time there was no hall beside it. After that, the lantern disappeared, too. I had many chances to climb up Mt. Koshikidake during hiking excursions in elementary, junior high and high school. I used to tell classmates these strange stories of my experiences there and made them tremble with fear.

The Osaka Exposition was held in 1970. Japan was in the middle of an era of high economic growth. Many attractive products were everywhere and people quickly forgot about the importance of spiritual matters. At that time, religious matters didn't matter to me. One day, I had the chance to visit Oregon in the United States as an exchange student. I happened to pass the examination which my friend should have taken. That was the time around the end of the hippy era and they barely survived in rural areas. In Oregon I visited a tepee commune where all the hippies were living together. Vietnam veterans were there too and were having a hard time getting along with their families. My host family were Mormons. I went to the church early in the morning and studied the Bible before heading off to school. Sometimes, I went along to parties with the other agricultural trainees from Japan and drank Colt 45s. I was such a bad boy for the Mormons but their religious life taught me a lot of lessons, though I did not realize them at the time.

I remained in the United States for one and a half years before returning to Japan. I finally graduated from senior high school at the age of 20. In those days, it was a matter of course that students had to graduate within a certain amount of time and progress onwards to the next phase of schooling. I however had already dropped out of regular life and took an extra year to graduate from university at the age of 25. I took a job at a TV station in Yamagata city. I quit however, because I was infuriated with the owner, who interfered with broadcasts by refusing to play news which went against several companies he was involved with. I transferred to another television station, and divorced the woman who was a relative of an executive of the newspaper which owned that television station.

The divorce trial at the court was a tragic comedy. Colleagues watched me with unconcealed curiosity. In such a dire situation, I began to go to a Tendai temple and attend the daily recitation service in order to recover some peace of mind. Even though I was a descendent of yamabushi, I was a lay practitioner. Fortunately, I was permitted to receive official ordination at the age of 36 and began post-ordination training.

Before beginning the training, one has to offer one thousand prostrations during which the hands, legs and head are pressed to the ground, in order to express repentance through the body to the Buddhas of the past, present, and future. In total, I offered three thousand prostrations over a period of three days. In addition to this I also performed prostrations to deities at the beginning and end of the initiation period. The first day and the second day were fine, but by the third day, I could not use the accelerator and brake pedals of my car because I had lost feeling in my legs.

During this time, I spent my days as a television reporter, taking lessons from my master on my days off. I entered the temple hall after work at around 9 or 10 pm and would spend the rest of the night practicing ritual, cleaning up each time upon completion. The water was freezing cold in winter and it would take me a long time to wipe the floor. I usually left the hall at around 4am and went back home to have a bath. When I was taught the Goma ceremony, I was given a large log and chopped the firewood myself. During this time, I would survive on only a couple of hours sleep a night. I was exhausted but had to commit to this kind of training for about a year.

During this practice, my master requested that I should begin begging for alms. Wearing black vestments and a wicker hat, I wandered from house-to-house reciting sutras to comfort the spirits of the dead. This took me roughly two years to complete and during this time I travelled across most of Yamagata prefecture. This training occurred at the same time as the Aum Shinrikyo terrorist incident of 1995, where a religious cult bombed a subway station in Tokyo with sarin gas. Because of this, people were very suspicious of religion and rejected anything religious. During this time some people would call the police and report me as a suspicious person. Another threw boiling water over me. I even encountered an old man in a village who approached me fearfully wearing an oxygen mask. One time I could not finish reciting the Heart Sutra because those in the household were embarrassed by it.

One day as I was leaving the temple, I thanked a fellow priest who had allowed me to park my car nearby. He had let me into the temple and served tea for two. The priest was a relative of my second marriage partner's friend. She called him to say thank you. He said to her that the two priests had practiced really well. I was alone, however. Who was with me? We were shocked and cried out in disbelief.

When I was finally permitted to

receive the official ordination ceremony and had my hair shaved, I arrived at work the next day and was asked to report to my manager's office. "You're fired!", he said. I asked for what reason and he replied, "Those with shaved heads are only inmates or *bozu* (monks)!" I replied that I had indeed become a monk. He made a wry face and let me out of the room with a gesture and I was allowed to keep my job. My boss later confronted me at a work party, stating "Religion is for the weak!". I laughed, because he was right. "But the weak cannot bear prejudices. I am not weak. I am determined to believe my religion," I cried in my mind.

My former master came from a lay family. He began training in Tendai after attending his best friend's funeral, where he encountered his figure floating right in front of him. He realised the existence of a different world and decided to become a Buddhist priest. He had a dynamic character and could perform ritual-procedures very well. One day I was called and asked to be his assistant in a certain ritual. This time however, he appeared and acted very differently. I asked him what he was performing the ritual prayer for. Expressionless, he answered that he was cursing someone. That person died two weeks later. My master told me to forget everything I saw and heard because it was just an accident and coincidence. It was from him that I completed my ritual training.

My father returned home after retiring and told me that he wanted to liquidate all the old documents related to our family's Shugendo practice. I took all of them and started translating them into modern Japanese from their original Chinese and Sanskrit characters. I had to research each character and painstakingly translate them one by one. One day, I had a strange dream where a monk taught me how to read certain parts and how to relate their meanings. As soon as I woke up, I wrote down what I had seen. I later had the meanings cross examined and they were all correct. I understood the content of these original scriptures and worked on restoring the old prayer procedures. Some of these were published as prayer books without the reserved manners.

I have been praying since I can remember. First it was like a children's game. Later, for a boy surrounded by entertainment and amusement, it became a pain to perform regular religious ceremonies. Busy with work and study, my religious activity began to wane. To tell you the truth, as a youth, prayer and ritual-practice was nothing cool for me. It seemed old-fashioned and behind the times.

At the age of 37 I was blessed with the birth of my daughter. Soon after however, we found out that she had developed retinopathy as a result of her pre-mature birth. In addition to this, my wife developed a tumour in her spine. I felt downcast, disheartened, heartbroken and hopeless. In this situation I blew away the dust of my old ritual-service books, which by now carried a musty odour. I prayed for my wife and daughter whenever I could snatch a spare moment. Fortunately, my daughter recovered. My wife, however lost the use of her legs due to secondary complications associated with the spinal surgery. The fulfillment I received from supporting and praying for them was something I had never felt before. This is what led me to keep hold of my ritual-prayer books and firmly dedicate myself to my family religion, Shugendo.

I had been practicing at Mt. Haguro, a sacred ground of Shugendo training in the Tohoku region, since the early 90s. Mt. Haguro is one of three mountains which together form Dewa Sanzan. My ancestor, whose name was Kokai Shonin, practiced at Dewa Sanzan and in particular at Mt. Yudono. He performed *mokujiki-gyo*, which is a type of training where only nuts, bark and grasses are consumed. At that time, Kannonji temple on Mt. Koshikidake was struck by lightning strike and burned down. He rebuilt the temple and later, in his old age, placed himself in an underground cavern, entered samadhi, and into his death prayed for people's relief and the flourishing of the Dharma. It is my desire to continue Kokai Shonin's wishes and revive the true spirit of Shugendo which my ancestors had taught and practiced.

That is why I practiced at Mt. Haguro, where there remains traces of the true spirit of Shugendo, under the guidance of master Shimazu Kokai.

I met many kinds of practitioners at Mt. Haguro. One old man I met was a soldier and staff officer in the Kwantung army during World War 2. He was there for atonement and to honour the memory of his fellow soldiers. A man who killed a person in an accidental car crash was there to heal the spirit of the victim. An old retiree came to prepare himself for the next world. A mysterious psychic served hidden amounts of food which surprised us and made us happy during our days of fasting. Some people drank too much of the *sake* served during ritual ceremonies which made them act in an inappropriate manner. Sometimes, foreign practitioners would join in and add a certain flavour to the events with their liveliness. One day, during our march down the mountain at the end of the retreat, a woman from Israel ran out from the procession towards her boyfriend to kiss him and everyone applauded. There were both moments of seriousness and comedy at the holy mountain in those days.

In reviving the Shugen of Kannonji, I was assisted along the way by other practitioners, just as in olden times. One example of this involves the head-priest from a temple known as Ajisaidera. This temple is famous for its flowers which bloom all the way up its stone steps. As a news reporter, I would often report on the flower-festival associated with this temple and in this way, I got to know and establish a good relationship with the head-priest. As time went on, he learned that I was a yamabushi of the Haguro sect, and further that my ancestors belonged to the Shugen lineage associated with Daigo-ji Sanboin; the same as his temple. Based on this connection, I shared with him the Shugen practices of my family's lineage. Seeing that these practices were the same as those of his temple, he taught me the unique single-offering style of practice which they were based on and helped me systematise them. This style of single-offering manner also exists in other denominations as an oral-tradition.

I was also granted permission by Daisendatsu Kokai Shimazu to transmit the ten-realms mountain-entry practice of Haguro Shugendo. Not everyone was happy with this decision, however, and it did cause some jealousy. At first, I thought of only transmitting the Haguro style, however every mountain carries a unique geography which reveals its own teachings. I knew Mt. Koshikidake like the back of my hand from climbing it over a 40-year period and knew exactly how to adjust the training to suit it.

Just before the age of 40, I reached a turning point in my life. My first Tendai master kept company with the yakuza and as I was a journalist, it was decided that I should part company with him. He was a serious and severe practitioner who had undertaken the 100-day *kaihogyo* practice of Mt. Hiei and diligently performed the Goma ceremony three times per day. The energy and dynamism of his practice is something that he passed on to me. At this point, I tried to quit the Tendai sect, however he would not let me. Following this, I transferred from the Sanmon School to the Jimon

School at Miidera under Reverend Fuke Eimei, who would later go on to become a high priest. During this time, I also received a recommendation to be introduced to a Yamagata-born priest by the name of Mitsunaga Tanno (his name before he was adopted). When I met him, he had just completed the thousand-day *kaihogyo* practice and emanated a severe and sharp atmosphere.

At the same time, some people began to come and study Shugendo under me. My daughter was not interested in succeeding our family temple and so I decided that I should broaden the gateway of my family temple and make it available to anyone who was interested. In the context of Shugendo's declining and aging membership, I also decided to reach out to foreign practitioners. This is also what led to this book.

Within Miidera, however, I was accosted for such activities, despite only wanting to transmit my family's teachings as a lay tradition. Thinking that I may cause trouble for my master, I decided to withdraw from Miidera. Within this context, I decided to try and have my temple activity officially recognised as a religious entity, something that became very difficult following the Aum Shinrikyo attacks. Many laughed at me thinking that it was an impossible pipe-dream. The road to receiving religious certification from the local government proved to be very difficult. However, due to my family history and record of temple activity, I was finally able to prove to them the validity of our temple lineage. In 2006, I finally established

Koshikidake Kannonji as a registered religious entity under the title of Koryu Shugen Honshu.

In Japan, practicing beyond the boundaries of sect-identities is the exception to the rule. Despite this, early on many practitioners did come to participate in the mountain-entry of Koshikidake which I organised, including fellow priests from Haguro. Things did not always run so smoothly, however.

I travelled to Shikoku Island and Kurashiki in Okayama at the request to provide teachings. Among my students, however, there were a number of suspicious people, including self-styled psychics, fortune readers, and practitioners from other sects. Our denomination began to spiral out of control. I was left disappointed by people who would take huge amounts of money from others after telling them strange stories about their karma and who had immoral relations with women. I saw and heard many disgusting things and became completely disheartened.

There was a fortune reader from the Kanto region who had roughly twenty students. I found out that she came to my temple after being kicked out of another temple. She was the person who told people strange stories regarding their karma in exchange for large sums of money. I kicked her out too and she sent two of her henchmen to threaten me. They said that they would get me fired, but I was able to handle the situation. One practitioner was a priest belonging to the Shingon sect. One day he had a thrombotic stroke in front of his believers. He sent me a message via fax afterwards stating that he had been punished by deities because he had become my disciple and that I should take personal responsibility for the incident. His ignorance really staggered me. He felt that he had lost face because he fell during his service and needed an excuse. Another practitioner was the owner of a group of companies and considered himself a good judge of character. He complained and rallied against me after I permitted one particular disciple he didn't like to attain a priestly qualification. I was forced to part with him.

There was a *qigong* therapist. He became my disciple, telling me that he was drawn to practice following the death of his girlfriend. However, he soon got together with another woman who was a self-styled psychic. The two of them travelled across Japan performing strange prayers for huge amounts of money. He claimed to be vegetarian but acted differently in private. I called him and asked him to choose between spiritual practice or his lifestyle. He chose women.

There was an owner of a worker-dispatch company. Every time he was supposed to come to study, he would say that he had a traffic accident, a flat tyre and so on. One day he said his employee died in a car accident, but I found out that he was working as a pimp. I agreed with him that this kind of work was 'worker-dispatch' and kicked him out.

There was a Shinto priest belonging to a Shinto sect on Shikoku Island. He became my disciple because he wanted to learn how to pray in a Buddhist way. After he studied the procedures, he wanted to learn, he began to send blackmail letters to other disciples he disliked. One of them took lots of medicine because she got such a shock from his blackmail. I kicked him out along with some other disciples who were his students. He was often proud of hard religious training such as climbing up precipitous mountains or waterfall asceticism in the middle of winter. But this kind of hard training turned him into an incarnation of conceit. Hard training does not always lead to an increase in one's humanity, humility or wisdom.

I learned to forget and forgive. A few years later, in part due to a fellow yamabushi and Tendai priest who practices at my temple, I was reintroduced to Dai Ajari Mitsunaga Tanno, who now went by the name Mitsunaga Kakudo. He remembered me and asked about my activities, knowing my life's ambition to revive my family's Shugen temple. When he asked me what my status was as a Tendai priest, I answered that I had tried to quit but that my ex-master had not allowed it to happen. He offered to check my status and found out that I was registered as a 'lost/missing priest'. Mitsunaga arranged to restore me as a priest belonging to his temple and took me on as his disciple, saying that this was something decided years earlier when I had first met him. Through this process, Mitsunaga Dai-Ajari also eventually became the honorary advisor of Koshikidake Kannonji.

聽我說者
知我心者

I would also like to share the first time I met Gaynor Sekimori at Haguro. Despite it being her first time there with us at Haguro, she already had the atmosphere of a veteran.

As a foreign woman going to great lengths to join in Haguro's mountain training, all of us had great respect for her. She joined in all of the proceedings and difficult practices without any hesitation, just as we did. This was amazing. In this way, I slowly introduced myself. She was also interested in my work as a television reporter and wanted to learn more about the historical character of Haguro's temple and shrine. I explained to her that I became a practitioner in order to revive my family's temple and the *shinbutsu-shugo* of Mount Koshikidake.

Without going too deep into Haguro's history, it is a fact that the tensions stemming from the Meiji period's separation orders remain today. As Shugendo was banned, the main temple on Haguro was converted into a Shrine and today Shugendo remains alive only at Kotakuji-Shozen'in. During my time as a reporter, the Shinto Haguro Shrine would accept me as a journalist, however as soon as I mentioned that I was a Yamabushi of Shozen'in (Haguro Shugen) the atmosphere would suddenly change. As a reporter, I would go to Haguro many times, for example in covering the Shonai 33 Kannon pilgrimage.

At Haguro, I was a rare figure in the sense that I was both a newscaster skilled in all aspects of film as well as being a practitioner. For this reason, Daisendatsu Kokai Shimazu, asked me to assist in documenting Haguro's autumn peak mountain-asceticism in order to preserve its fragile existence for future generations. He initially asked me to do this using a home video camera to go along with some lectures he had been planning. I couldn't believe it and with my mouth wide open, I could barely say the words 'Seriously!?' I knew this was a rare once-in-a-lifetime opportunity and that it had to be done properly. For this reason, I contacted my friend who runs Visual Folklore, a company which specialises in the documentation of religious ritual and folk-customs. He had also taken part in Haguro's mountain entry and knew how infinitely valuable this opportunity was, considering that Haguro Shugen had always maintained its secrecy. He agreed to take on the project, however we lacked the funds to proceed.

For this reason, we had to apply for a government grant connected with the media organisation Japan Broadcasting Corporation (NHK). To get a chance at this grant, we had to quickly come up with a script, and so for three sleepless days and nights I put together a script which should have taken a week to finish. We received the grant and were able to go ahead with filming. With this grant, Visual Folklore were able to arrange a crew and three skilled cameramen. One of the cameramen had experience covering footage of a famous Mt. Everest mountain-climber, one was well-known for his coverage of professional rally-car racing and one was a documentary cameraman who was experienced with HD cameras; the most advanced cameras available at the time. With this team, we were able to cover the entirety of the mountain-training of Haguro, round the clock. While the cameramen changed shift every eight hours, I was required to be on 24 hours a day. By the end of the nine days, I suffered from hematuria. In the end, Visual Folklore offered to turn this footage into a documentary suitable for screening and my master was very happy with the editing and the final result. It remains a moment of great pride and joy for me. Some practitioners complained saying that Haguro Shugen's practices should be kept secret. However, from my perspective, the outcome of this narrowminded attitude means that the world only ever hears the Shinto side of Haguro's story.

As I mentioned, the grant came from NHK and the documentary was going to be aired officially on NHK's channel. As I worked for a different media company, I was concerned about the potential for tension to arise. For this reason, I requested that I be listed as simply a supporter so as to avoid any trouble. Although I requested that my name not be advertised as being involved with the documentary itself, my involvement was later found out and I was heavily reprimanded by my company. I didn't care, which made them even madder, and so I was demoted from being a reporter to working in the control room; a job which would mostly involve long night shifts.

February 20th, 2014 was the day before I was told that I would be working in a new role in the main master control room of the television company. I visited my master on this day. I had been working as a news reporter for more than 25 years and told him that I was greatly disheartened with how the company was treating me. He told me that being made to do something that I had not expected was a good thing and that experiencing a different view of life should be treated as a gift. After this conversation, I decided to go ahead with working in the new section as a shift worker.

This was an incredibly difficult change for me, however the work itself was easy. I started my career at the television station forty years earlier at the tail end of the film-camera. The film-camera required great skill to operate as the maximum length of ten feet of film had to be expertly used so as to capture all the necessary footage. One set of film would only last three minutes. This means that the camera operator had only three minutes to cover everything, and it required great skill to select the right scenes. Today, however, we have the luxury of using cameras with basically no time limit. Today's camera operators have infinite takes to capture a single event which the old film-camera operators would have to capture in just three minutes.

With this background, the work was not difficult for me, and editing was simple because of my experience in capturing scenes with the film-camera. What would take the new camera operators one hour would take me less than fifteen minutes. Those newer to the work wondered how I was able to work so efficiently. Further, my new nightshift work basically saw me acting as an overseer, and, despite the night shift, the new roster meant that I would have two and a half days free for every three days of work. There were rarely any errors and programs would go ahead without any issue. This combined with my skill with the camera meant I had a lot of free time. This situation basically allowed me to work on my religious activities and the goal of reviving my family temple full-time, with my workplace as the headquarters of operations. My fellow employees knew that I was demoted for silly reasons and supported me in my activity and in this way my trouble was suddenly transformed into a blessing.

As I mentioned, my wife became wheelchair bound following complications associated with surgery. Following an incident where I was confronted and ashamed by the judgemental stare of a high school teacher while at a shopping centre, I decided that I would take my wife everywhere with me. Prior to this, I had no knowledge about how society worked for people with disabilities. To know the situation of people with disabilities became a wonderful chance to deepen and broaden my way of thinking about life and the world. I've experienced many such things which left me disheartened and devastated, however these situations sometimes reveal and open things up to deeper understanding. The base of Shugendo's ten realms practice is that we all start on the platform of the hell realm. In this way suffering, troubles and the depths of despair can be a bridge. If we can find a way based on our sorrows and suffering, it will make life wider and deeper rather than narrower. This is also the teaching of En no Gyoja.

Many people knock at the door of Shugendo in search of challenging themselves. The idea of 'challenge' in Shugendo however has nothing to do with a lone-hero image. In Shugendo, we are challenged to take actions which take us beyond our habitual thoughts, beyond our narrow thinking, beyond our separateness, meeting our weaknesses in order to encounter others. Practice does not mean becoming a superhero who feels no pain. Seeing into our own weakness can be a way to see into our troubles. Among weakness and hardship, we can also find the blossoming of kindness and gentleness. These are things that we can then share with others. This attitude of a lone hero may look good in the cinema, but it doesn't let us see the margins of life. To live with others, we have to be able to share and accept our weaknesses. This becomes the power of helping one another.

During mountain training, the platform of practice is devised and adjusted so that everyone can join, regardless of ability. If people came to the mountain with this kind of lone-hero attitude, we would be unable to maintain mountain training, which requires all practitioners to rely upon one another. In this way, mountain training teaches us many things. What is strength in humanity? To complete mountain training without someone going missing or getting injured requires great effort. In this way, it becomes a precious treasure for everyone, something which they go on to share with others when they return from the mountain. Staying only in the mountain is not Shugendo, which involves returning and being welcomed back into society to share the blessings of practice. If those with a lone-hero mindset want to become strong, they should go to the gym. However, even these kinds of people learn something from mountain-training.

Up until now, I have organized our network beyond the lines of sects, denominations and nationalities. I am certain that the deities have been assisting me in introducing the ecstasy of Shugendo to the world and I have dedicated myself to making this gift available to all, including talented people outside of Japan. Shugendo reminds us that existence is greater than just us. Through practice, we forget ourselves and capture an aspect of the universe. It is for this reason that I believe we should make many doors to lead to the gates of Shugendo.

Post-script

The most difficult aspect of reviving my temple's Shugendo has been the reconstruction and revival of ritual practice.

When Japan was ushered into the modern era during the Meiji period, Shugendo was prohibited and its spiritual concepts were destroyed. Hand in hand with this, in my view, was the aim to establish the emperor as a priestly king. Shugendo, with its myriads of divinities, was an obstacle in the way of this tide of modernity and Shugendo temples that were associated with kami shrines were ordered to submit their images and ritual documents to be destroyed. This is how Shugendo lost its unique identity. Not all documents were burnt, however. Some, like those of my family, narrowly escaped by being hidden.

I moved to Yamagata from Hokkaido when I was ten years old to be with my grandmother, who taught me a basic recitation service. At this time however I had no knowledge of esoteric ritual. I became a practitioner of Haguro Shugen and at the age of thirty-six I was also ordained in the Tendai sect. This was the beginning of my path of revival. There was another problem, however. Many Shugen sects have started a process of reviving their ritual systems, but in my eyes many of them carried forward incorrect interpretations, or at least transmitted interpretations which were very different to those written down in the commentaries of my family tradition. When I raised issues of interpretation, I was rarely listened to because I was just an obscure, unknown practitioner. I can say that many ritual systems lack this kind of deeper interpretation. When I was teaching at a seminar in Kyoto, one priest asked how I knew about the meaning of certain ritual procedures which he had only received as a formality as part of the official transmission of teaching (*denpo kanjo*). In this climate of empty ritual, some rituals have come to lose their substance, and teachings reduced to questions of ranking.

I have been in training as a practitioner of Shugendo since the age of ten, though I quit during the temptations of youth in my early twenties. Following the bitter end of my wild youth, I once again picked up religious activities. I gave up eating and sleeping in my resolvc to revive Shugendo, all the while working full time at a TV station. I was an anchor on a news program for several years. There is a popular perception that TV presenters have a fake character and deceive their audiences. In Japanese, there is a phrase, 'hora-fuki' which means to blow the conch-trumpet. In popular jargon, it means to be a braggart, making lots of noise without any meaning. Anyway, I can say that I blow the conch shell for real!

I went through hell and back to revive the teachings and the power of prayer carried through my family temple, some taking almost a decade to come to fruition. The old style of Shugendo in the Dewa region was based on a single offering procedure called *kataku-saho*. This may be characterised as an unsophisticated style of esoteric ritual, however these procedures were highly specialised and secret. From the outside, it may seem like an uncouth form of ritual practice. However, it has a delicate structure, and its performance requires severe training. Due to its simplicity, it reflects the capacity of the practitioner directly like a mirror. Among the ritual manuals passed down within my family there are many which are worn out, including ritual methods dedicated to divinities such as Izuna, Shogun Jizo and Dakini-ten, all in the *kataku-saho* style. This reveals that my ancestors performed this kind of ritual practice much more than other kinds. Seeing the prevalence of this ritual system gave me the sense of a very strong power.

As part of my role as a TV reporter I had the opportunity to build relationships and visit many temples, often to cover stories related to local festivals. As part of this process, I met a Dewa Shugen priest whose temple had passed on the *kataku-saho* style of practice. His temple belongs to Daigo-ji, which is one of the foundation temples of Shugen-shu. As it happens, this was also the sect which my ancestors belonged to. Through my persistence I was permitted to learn this practice from him, and to my surprise many parts of the ritual manuals were the same as those found in my family's documents. With great fervour, I constantly visited his temple to study this style of ritual. As my background is in Tendai, I perform procedures and etiquette according to the Homan-ryu style. The arrangement of implements in the *kataku-saho* style however is completely different from Homan-ryu and other forms of esoteric Buddhist ritual. When other priests view the *kataku-saho* arrangement they do not understand it and think we are performing some kind of odd, obscure style of prayer. This is proof however of the destruction and marginalising of Shugendo. It is a sad thing.

In my opinion, reviving Shugendo requires a clear emphasis on En no Gyoja. In our lineage, En no Gyoja is considered an emanation of Sakyamuni, manifested to teach the essence of the Dharma. Whereas Mahavairocana is a universal existence, En no Gyoja was a flesh and blood human who existed on our planet. Shugendo is a religion deeply intertwined with humanity. As practitioners, we share the troubles of others and bring them to the platform of Shugendo training, and as practitioners, we can face the common problems of our everyday lives with pangs in our hearts. That is, Vairocana and human beings stand side by side.

What can be said of the relevance of En no Gyoja's teachings for the world today? Shugendo contains enormous possibilities beyond the boundaries of its conception as a mere religion. It is a time capsule which points to the ancient history and memory of humankind. The mountain training of death and rebirth based on the ten realms, five stages and three-crossings, is a practice which establishes a true path of brushing up the mind. This is the foundation which En no Gyoja put into motion over 1000 years ago. Above all, Shugendo is a form of religious training, but we can also say that its purpose extends into a dignified way of life relevant to the concerns of the world today. Our concepts surrounding what we now separately refer to as 'nature' are completely different when compared to ancient times. We now live in a world where the way of life is completely altering the life-giving systems of this planet. In another way, we can say that the beautiful order of the universe, the harmony of the five elements and of yin and yang are being disturbed. Going forward into the future guided only by this kind of behaviour, we are facing something well beyond human understanding. In this situation, I worry for the future we will face. I have great faith, however, that the legacy left by En no Gyoja may help in some way to recover from the irregular order of our times. The way of En no Gyoja is worth learning and practicing, not only as a religious path, but also as a method to be reborn with the heart-mind which recognises that we are true aspects and members of this universe.

The expression *sato yamabushi* refers to a married practitioner of Shugendo who manages a village temple as its priest. The *sato yamabushi* prays for people and travels into the mountains regularly to practice. In addition to this, the *sato yamabushi* has the character of being an upstanding member of the community, that is, a good citizen. I'm not sure if I can refer to myself as a good citizen, but I can say that I am a typical *sato yamabushi*. The *sato yamabushi* lacks the prestige of having a glorious temple. Instead, their religious activities take place in the everyday reality of an ordinary household. In this household however there is a room dedicated to religious activities. Many people come and go to this household to be touched by the blessing of prayer. Intimately connected with the local community, *sato yamabushi* spend their life at the front-line of ordinary life where people come and bring a wide variety of troubles and tribulations to them. The *sato yamabushi* must respond to all of them and must possess the capacity to rescue them from the bewilderment of *samsara* (birth-death). I can say that this is my life.

In terms of what the future holds, I have inherited many rituals which are characteristic of *shinbutsu-shugo*, that is, the combination of Shintoism and Buddhism. There are many practices, ranging from simple to difficult. *Sato yamabushi*, including my ancestors, used a wide variety of methods and skilful means to accomplish their tasks. My current interest lies in astrology as another tool. I am currently working on reviving systems of astrology as they were practiced in the past. This is a gateway to studying the logic of the universe, and it is my belief that the lunar calendar and various ephemera all share the underlying logic of Shugendo. One of my future projects will be to revive and share this system. I have studied various forms of divination, including four pillar astrology, esoteric Buddhist astrology as well as western astrology. I believe they all share the same root in the same cosmic laws. Recently I have been teaching my philosophy related to astrology which also reveals the underlying thought of Shugendo. Both esoteric Buddhism and Shugendo share the idea of the universe revealing the truths of Buddhism. As a modern *sato yamabushi,* I have also been interested in the role of technology and have attempted to make full use of the internet and social-media. As part of this process, I have been able to connect with people all over the world and livestream my prayers and religious activities for those who request them using six cameras. My next dream has seen my eyes curiously looking to the virtual world for answers to Shugendo's continual survival, and in particular, what the Metaverse may have to offer.

Acknowledgements

I am no saint. I was not a capable employee for the company that employed me. Yes, as a yamabushi, I am an eccentric person. You may have read religious books written by high-priests, scholars and others who have profound knowledge. I am sorry; I cannot be counted among such people. This book is not an academic study, but rather is based on my own direct experience as a yamabushi.

I am not a perfect man. My younger years were spent in debauchery. I was dragged into the world of Shugendo despite my hesitations at the time, not knowing its real value. However, many people led me to realise that Shugendo was my life-long task. My grandmother encouraged and pushed me to succeed our family lineage when I was only nine years old. As a child, I moved to Yamagata by myself to live with my grandmother from Hokkaido, where my father was working as a high school teacher. Living in this strongly religious situation, I recoiled and became distracted due to the foolishness of my youth. By the time I realized my life's purpose, my grandmother was going senile. I deeply reflected on my foolishness which gave way to endless gratitude for her patience. My grandmother kept safe our family's Shugendo documents, which I would go on to utilize in my efforts to revive pre-modern Shugendo. My grandmother's name was Shiu, which she would write using the hiragana characters, 'しう'. It is only recently that that I found out that the character used to write her name was '舟',

which means ship. With this, I realized that she was the ship which ferried me to the world of Shugendo. If this ship didn't exist, I would have never travelled on this life path. My efforts to re-establish Kannonji temple as Koryu Shugen Honshu was miscarried several times. I expelled a self-styled psychic who caused great trouble in our order. She sent her followers to threaten me. Another tried to organize a takeover of the sect. A famous self-styled 'ninja' martial artist used some basic teachings I gave on Shugendo as a vehicle for his vanity. One senior practitioner was found to be involved with a strange black magic cult and stealing our rituals. There are many examples of this kind of difficult situation. Each time, I was left flustered and disheartened. However, I also had disciples with good roots who encouraged and supported me.

I began posting information on Shugendo on the internet thinking that it would be seen as nothing but absolute nonsense. To my surprise, some people caught wind of my voice and travelled across the sea, curious to find out what I was talking about. That must have been a tough decision. Their actions encouraged me and made me realise that Shugendo has the potential to be a gift for people across the world. It is to them that I owe this English introduction.

Yamabushi used to organise mountain pilgrimages to sacred sites as a kind of rite of passage. People could join regardless of their denomination or beliefs. In this way, Shugendo was the platform upon which all other religions in Japan would go on to express themselves. If this is true, I do not see any reason why even Christians, for example, could not join this pilgrimage towards the inner spiritual world.

I started writing this book in 2012, with the hope of introducing genuine Shugendo practice. In Japan, no one believed that the origin of Shugendo lay in the harmony between Shinto and Buddhism, because that reality no longer exists in modern day Japan. The denominations that now profess Shugendo all have a shared history of being decimated in the early years of the Meiji period, an experience during which Shugendo was both absorbed and broken apart. In my view, many modern priests and monks acted as Trojan Horses in continuing this decimation.

The road towards getting this book published has been difficult and complicated, and plagued with issues. Salvaging this manuscript from previous editions which were marked by various kinds of issues has proved a great challenge. Now, this ship that I have been boarding is gently growing in size little by little. It may take more time to make more space to let more people in, but I will sail this ship to wherever it is invited to come.

I deeply appreciate my students and all the people who have been supporting my voyage. In particular, I owe endless gratitude to master Kokai Shimazu, previous head-priest of Haguro Shugen Honshu, who gave me permission to continue the profound teachings and practices of mountain-entry and the ten-realms training. I would like to give thanks to my disciple Jisho Schroer for heading this project and rescuing it from disaster. His efforts and in-person interviews with me formed the basis for much of this book. Thank you also to my disciples Eikai Ip, Meido Moore and Kanjin Cederman for their assistance and ongoing encouragement. A special thankyou goes to Dr. Gaynor Sekimori, who graced this simple book with her wisdom stemming from her status as both a world-renowned scholar and Shugen practitioner. I appreciate all the help and support provided by my disciples and my wife, Kiyomi. I dedicate this book to the successive line of yamabushi who safeguarded Shugendo through the turbulence of the Meiji period and to those who discovered, inherited and transmitted Shugendo into the present. I hope this book will act as a gate for seekers across the world.

Printed in Dunstable, United Kingdom

73948073R00107